United States

HARCOURT BRACE SOCIAL STUDIES

ASSESSMENT PROGRAM

HARCOURT BRACE & COMPANY

Orlando Atlanta Austin Boston San Francisco Chicago Dallas

New York Toronto London

Visit The Learning Site at http://www.hbschool.com

Printed in the United States of America

ISBN 0-15-312122-X

5 6 7 8 9 10 022 02 01

CONTENTS

Overview

The assessment program in *Harcourt Brace Social Studies* allows all learners many opportunities to show what they know and can do. It provides you with ongoing information about each student's understanding of social studies.

The assessment program is designed around the Assessment Model in the chart below. The multi-dimensional framework is balanced between teacher-based and student-based assessments. The teacher-based strand typically involves assessments in which the teacher evaluates a student's work as evidence of his or her understanding of social studies content and ability to think critically about it. The teacher-based strand consists of two components: Formal Assessment and Performance Assessment.

The student-based strand involves assessments that invite the student to become a partner in the assessment process. These student-based assessments encourage students to reflect on and evaluate their own efforts. The student-based strand also consists of two components: Student Self-Evaluation and Portfolio Assessment.

The fifth component in the *Harcourt Brace Social Studies* assessment program is Informal Assessment. This essential component is listed in the center of the Assessment Model because it is the "glue" that binds together the other types of assessment.

HARCOURT BRACE SOCIAL STUDIES
Assessment Model
Grades 4–6

Teacher-Based	Student-Based

Formal Assessment
• Lesson Reviews
• Chapter Reviews
• Chapter Tests
• Unit Reviews
• Unit Assessment
   Standard Tests
   Performance Tasks
	Student Self-Evaluation
	• Individual End-of-Project Summary
	• Group End-of-Project Checklist
	• Individual End-of-Unit Checklist

Informal Assessment
• REVIEW Questions
• Think and Apply
• Visual Summary
• Social Studies Skills Checklist

Teacher-Based	Student-Based
Performance Assessment • Show What You Know • Cooperative Learning Workshop • Scoring Rubric for Individual Projects • Scoring Rubric for Group Projects • Scoring Rubric for Presentations	**Portfolio Assessment** • Student-Selected Work Samples • Teacher-Selected Assessments • A Guide to My Social Studies Portfolio • Individual End-of-Unit Checklist • Social Studies Portfolio Summary • Portfolio Family Response

Description of Assessment Components and Materials in This Booklet

Informal Assessment
Informal Assessment is central to the *Harcourt Brace Social Studies* assessment program. Ultimately, it is your experienced eye that will provide the most comprehensive assessment of students' growth. This booklet provides a checklist to help you evaluate the social studies skills that your students demonstrate in the classroom (pages 4–5).

Formal Assessment
This booklet provides Chapter and Unit Assessments (beginning on page 15) to help you reinforce and assess students' understanding of ideas that are developed during instruction. Each Unit Assessment includes standard tests and performance tasks. Answers to assessment items and suggested scores are provided in the Answer Key (beginning on page 175).

Student Self-Evaluation
Student self-evaluation encourages students to reflect on and monitor their own gains in social studies knowledge, development of group skills, and changes in attitude. In this booklet, you will find checklists for both individual and group self-evaluation (pages 6–8).

Performance Assessment
Social studies literacy involves more than just what students know. It is concerned with how they think and do things. This booklet provides scoring rubrics to help you evaluate individual projects, group projects, and student presentations (pages 9–11).

Portfolio Assessment
For portfolio assessment, students create their own portfolios, which may also contain a few required or teacher-selected papers. Included in this booklet are support materials to assist you and your students in developing portfolios and in using them to evaluate growth in social studies (pages 12–14).

Rating Scale
3 Proficient
2 Adequate
1 Improvement needed
☐ Not enough opportunity to observe

Students' Names

BASIC STUDY SKILLS

Map and Globe Skills

understanding globes					
understanding the purpose and use of maps					
comparing maps with globes					
comparing maps with photographs					
understanding map symbols					
understanding directional terms and finding direction					
understanding and measuring distance					
understanding and finding location					

Chart and Graph Skills

understanding and using pictographs					
understanding and using charts and diagrams					
understanding and using bar graphs					
understanding and using calendars and time lines					
understanding and using tables and schedules					

Reading and Research Skills

locating and gathering information					
using context clues to understand vocabulary					
using illustrations/objects to understand vocabulary					
grouping and categorizing words (semantic maps)					
understanding facts and main ideas					
understanding artifacts and documents					
understanding photographs and picture illustrations					
understanding fine art					
understanding safety and information symbols					
making observations					
asking questions					
expressing ideas in various ways					
writing and dictating					
speaking and listening					

(continued)

Reading and Research Skills (continued)

dramatizing and role-playing simulations						
listing and ordering						
constructing and creating						
displaying, charting, and drawing						

CITIZENSHIP SKILLS

Critical Thinking Skills

identifying cause-and-effect relationships						
following sequence and chronology						
classifying and grouping information						
summarizing						
synthesizing						
making inferences and generalizations						
forming logical conclusions						
understanding and evaluating point of view and perspective						
evaluating and making judgments						
predicting likely outcomes						
making thoughtful choices and decisions						
solving problems						

Participation Skills

working with others						
resolving conflicts						
acting responsibly						
keeping informed						
respecting rules and laws						
participating in a group or community						
respecting people with differing points of view						
assuming leadership						
being willing to follow						
making decisions and solving problems in a group setting						
understanding patriotic and cultural symbols						

Name _____

Date _____

To Sum It Up

You can tell about and evaluate your project by
completing these sentences.

1. My project was about _____

_____

2. These people helped me as I worked on my project: _____

_____

_____

3. I gathered information from these sources: _____

_____

_____

4. The most important thing I learned from doing this project is

_____

_____

_____

5. I will use what I have learned _____

_____

6. My evaluation of my project is _____

_____

I think I deserve this evaluation because _____

_____

7. I would like to say _____

_____

_____

Name _____ Date _____

Group Members _____

How Did Your Group Do?

Mark the number that tells the score you think
your group deserves.

How well did your group	High		Low
1. plan for the activity?	3	2	1
2. carry out group plans?	3	2	1
3. listen to and show respect for each member?	3	2	1
4. share the work?	3	2	1
5. solve problems without the teacher's help?	3	2	1
6. make use of available resources?	3	2	1
7. record and organize information?	3	2	1
8. communicate what was learned?	3	2	1
9. demonstrate critical and creative thinking?	3	2	1
10. set up for the activity and clean up afterward?	3	2	1

Think about each question below and write a short answer.

11. What did your group do best?_____

_____

_____

12. What can you do to help your group do better work? _____

_____

_____

13. What did your group like best about the activity? _____

_____

_____

Name _____ Date _____

Unit Title _____

Here's What I Think

Decide whether you agree or disagree with each statement below. Circle the word that tells what you think. If you are not sure, circle the question mark. Use the back of the sheet for comments.

1. This unit was very interesting.	**Agree**	**?**	**Disagree**
2. I learned a lot.	**Agree**	**?**	**Disagree**
3. I enjoyed working in groups.	**Agree**	**?**	**Disagree**
4. I enjoyed working alone.	**Agree**	**?**	**Disagree**
5. I felt comfortable giving my ideas and raising questions.	**Agree**	**?**	**Disagree**
6. I was cooperative and helped others learn.	**Agree**	**?**	**Disagree**
7. I contributed my fair share to group work.	**Agree**	**?**	**Disagree**
8. I am getting better at making decisions and solving problems.	**Agree**	**?**	**Disagree**
9. I worked on social studies at home and in the community as well as at school.	**Agree**	**?**	**Disagree**
10. I understood the ideas in this unit.	**Agree**	**?**	**Disagree**
11. I think I am doing well in social studies.	**Agree**	**?**	**Disagree**

Think about each question below and write a short answer.

12. What did you like best in this unit? Tell why. _____

_____

13. What is something you can do better now than you could do before?

_____

14. What is something you understand now that you didn't understand before?

_____

_____

Name _____ Date _____

Check the indicators that describe the student's performance on a project or task. The section with the most check marks indicates the student's overall score.

4 Point Score Indicators: The student
_____ gathers a lot of relevant, accurate information.
_____ shows thorough understanding of content.
_____ demonstrates strong social studies skills.
_____ exhibits outstanding insight/creativity.
_____ communicates ideas clearly and effectively.

3 Point Score Indicators: The student
_____ gathers sufficient relevant, accurate information.
_____ shows adequate understanding of content.
_____ demonstrates adequate social studies skills.
_____ exhibits reasonable insight/creativity.
_____ communicates most ideas clearly and effectively.

2 Point Score Indicators: The student
_____ gathers limited relevant, accurate information.
_____ shows partial understanding of content.
_____ demonstrates weak social studies skills.
_____ exhibits limited insight/creativity.
_____ communicates a few ideas clearly and effectively.

1 Point Score Indicators: The student
_____ fails to gather relevant, accurate information.
_____ shows little or no understanding of content.
_____ does not demonstrate social studies skills.
_____ does not exhibit insight/creativity.
_____ has difficulty communicating ideas clearly and effectively.

Overall score for the project _____

Comments:

Group _____ Date _____

Check the indicators that describe a group's performance on a project or task. The section with the most check marks indicates the group's overall score.

4 Point Score Indicators: The group
_____ makes outstanding use of resources.
_____ shows thorough understanding of content.
_____ works very cooperatively; contributions are about equal.
_____ displays strong decision-making/problem-solving skills.
_____ exhibits outstanding insight/creativity.
_____ communicates ideas clearly and effectively.

3 Point Score Indicators: The group
_____ makes good use of resources.
_____ shows adequate understanding of content.
_____ works cooperatively; contributions are nearly equal.
_____ displays adequate decision-making/problem-solving skills.
_____ exhibits reasonable insight/creativity.
_____ communicates most ideas clearly and effectively.

2 Point Score Indicators: The group
_____ makes limited use of resources.
_____ shows partial understanding of content.
_____ works cooperatively at times, but contributions are unequal.
_____ displays weak decision-making/problem-solving skills.
_____ exhibits limited insight/creativity.
_____ communicates some ideas clearly and effectively.

1 Point Score Indicators: The group
_____ makes little or no use of resources.
_____ fails to show understanding of content.
_____ does not work cooperatively; some members don't contribute.
_____ does not display decision-making/problem-solving skills.
_____ does not exhibit insight/creativity.
_____ has difficulty communicating ideas clearly and effectively.

Overall score for the project _____

Comments:

Name _____ Date _____

Check the indicators that describe the student's or group's presentation. The section with the most check marks indicates the overall score for the presentation.

4 Point Score Indicators: The presentation
_____ shows evidence of extensive research/reflection.
_____ demonstrates thorough understanding of content.
_____ is exceptionally clear and effective.
_____ exhibits outstanding insight/creativity.
_____ is of high interest to the audience.

3 Point Score Indicators: The presentation
_____ shows evidence of adequate research/reflection.
_____ demonstrates acceptable understanding of content.
_____ is, overall, clear and effective.
_____ shows reasonable insight/creativity.
_____ is of general interest to the audience.

2 Point Score Indicators: The presentation
_____ shows evidence of limited research/reflection.
_____ demonstrates partial understanding of content.
_____ is clear and effective in some parts but not in others.
_____ shows limited insight/creativity.
_____ is of some interest to the audience.

1 Point Score Indicators: The presentation
_____ shows little or no evidence of research/reflection.
_____ demonstrates poor understanding of content.
_____ is, for the most part, unclear and ineffective.
_____ does not show insight/creativity.
_____ is of little interest to the audience.

Overall score for the presentation _____

Comments:

Name _____ Date _____

A Guide to
My Social Studies Portfolio

What Is in My Portfolio	Why I Chose It
1.	
2.	
3.	
4.	
5.	
6.	

I organized my portfolio this way because _____

_____

_____

_____

Name _____ Date _____

Goals	Evidence and Comments
1. Growth in understanding social studies concepts	_____ _____ _____
2. Growth in building social studies skills	_____ _____ _____
3. Growth in thinking critically and creatively	_____ _____ _____
4. Growth in developing democratic values and civic responsibility	_____ _____ _____

Summary of Portfolio Assessment

For This Review			Since Last Review		
Excellent	**Good**	**Fair**	**Improving**	**About the Same**	**Not as Good**

Date _____

Dear Family Members,

Here are samples of social studies work that your child and I have chosen for portfolio assessment. Please ask your child to explain what he or she has done. Then write a short note to your child in the space below, telling your thoughts about what you have seen. Please have your child bring the portfolio, with your note, back to school.

Sincerely,

_____

Dear _____ ,

Family Member

_____

Chapter Test 1

Part One: Test Your Understanding

DIRECTIONS: *Circle the letter of the best answer.*

1. During the last Ice Age, the oceans became shallower because
  - **A.** the seawater evaporated.
  - **B.** the ice in the glaciers started to melt.
  - **C.** it did not rain for many years.
  - **D.** much of the water was locked up in glaciers.

2. Beringia is the name of the land bridge that once connected
  - **A.** North America and Turtle Island.
  - **B.** Alaska and California.
  - **C.** Asia and North America.
  - **D.** Asia and Siberia.

3. Indian peoples tell of their beliefs about the world and their place in it through their
  - **A.** origin stories.
  - **B.** theories.
  - **C.** mesas.
  - **D.** technology.

4. People were able to keep a regular surplus of food after the development of
  - **A.** earthworks.
  - **B.** agriculture.
  - **C.** the atlatl.
  - **D.** culture.

5. The Olmec culture is known as the "mother civilization" of the Americas because
  - **A.** Olmec farmers were the first farmers to grow corn in the Americas.
  - **B.** the Olmecs built large earthwork mounds in their cities.
  - **C.** the Olmecs were the first people to live in the Americas.
  - **D.** Olmec culture influenced the cultures of so many later groups.

6. The people who built pueblos were the
  - **A.** Olmecs.
  - **B.** Mississippians.
  - **C.** Anasazi.
  - **D.** Hopewells.

(continued)

DIRECTIONS: *Fill in the blank with the correct word or words from the list below.*

adobe	agriculture	archaeologists
atlatl	band	clan
cultural diffusion	kitchen	kiva
nomads	tribes	

7. A small group of people who work together to do things, such as hunt, is

called a _____.

8. People who wander from place to place and have no settled home are

called _____.

9. Scientists who study the cultures of people who lived long ago are

known as _____.

10. The _____ was a tool used to throw a spear.

11. _____ developed when people began to plant and grow their
own food.

12. _____ takes place when people of different cultures begin to
exchange ideas and goods.

13. _____ is a kind of sandy clay that can be dried into bricks
and used for building.

14. The _____ was a special underground room used by the
Anasazi for their religious services.

(continued)

Part Two: Test Your Skills

DIRECTIONS: *Use the information in the time line to answer the following questions.*

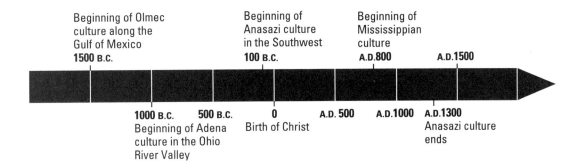

15. Which of these took place before the birth of Christ—the beginning of the Anasazi culture or the beginning of the Mississippian culture?

_____

16. The Hopewell culture developed in the area between the present-day states of New York and Kentucky around 300 B.C. If you were to place this event on the time line, would you place it before or after the birth of Christ?

_____

17. Which of these events took place after the birth of Christ—the beginning of the Olmec culture or the end of the Anasazi culture? _____

_____

18. When was the end of the Anasazi culture? _____

19. Which culture began at a time that was closer to the present—the Adenas or the Anasazi? _____

20. Which event took place earlier—the beginning of the Olmec culture or the birth of Christ? _____

(continued)

Part Three: Apply What You Have Learned

DIRECTIONS: *Complete each of the following activities.*

21. Arrival Theories

Archaeologists disagree as to when early people first arrived in the Americas. In the spaces below, give one argument that supports the Early Arrival Theory and one argument that supports the Late Arrival Theory.

EARLY ARRIVAL THEORY	LATE ARRIVAL THEORY

22. The Development of Agriculture

The development of agriculture resulted in many changes in the ways of life of early civilizations. Describe three of the changes in how people lived or how they made their living after agriculture was developed. Use one sentence for each change.

_____

_____

_____

23. Essay

The cultures of the early Indian peoples were affected by the environment in which they lived. Write one paragraph explaining how changes in the weather and climate of their environments affected these early peoples.

Chapter Test 2

Part One: Test Your Understanding

DIRECTIONS: *Circle the letter of the best answer.*

1. The Indian peoples who got most of their food from the rivers and oceans close to their homes were the
    - A. Chinooks and Makahs.
    - B. Hopis and Navajos.
    - C. Iroquois and Cherokees.
    - D. Mayas and Aztecs.

2. Why did the Chinooks develop a special language?
    - A. They needed a language for their religious ceremonies.
    - B. They wanted to teach their children about their culture.
    - C. They wanted a language in which to tell their origin stories.
    - D. They needed a language to make trade easier.

3. The Makahs did **not** use parts of the whales
    - A. for food.
    - B. to make oil to burn as fuel.
    - C. to make ropes and bags.
    - D. to make totem poles.

4. Pueblo family members needed to store surplus food so they could
    - A. barter with wandering tribes.
    - B. eat when there was a drought.
    - C. feed the kachina dancers.
    - D. survive the long, cold winter.

5. How did the Iroquois stop the fighting among neighboring tribes?
    - A. They moved to the southwestern part of the United States.
    - B. They held a potlatch ceremony and invited all the tribes.
    - C. They formed a confederation.
    - D. They invited all the tribes to play a game of Little War.

6. The Indian people who adopted ideas from the Mayas and went on to build a large empire were the
    - A. Aztecs.
    - B. Anasazi.
    - C. Makahs.
    - D. Olmecs.

(continued)

DIRECTIONS: *Fill in the blank with the correct word or words from the list below.*

band	barter	buffalo
city-state	clan	confederation
kachinas	kitchen	kiva
slavery	totem pole	tribe

7. A _____ is a group of families that are related to one another.

8. People went to the Dalles from all over the Northwest to exchange goods, or _____ .

9. The carved post that shows the history of a family is a _____ .

10. _____ are the guardian spirits of the Hopis.

11. The Plains Indians made clothes, tools, weapons, and food from the _____ they hunted.

12. A _____ is a loose group of governments.

13. Each Mayan _____ had its own ruler and its own government.

14. Holding people against their will and making them carry out orders is called _____ .

(continued)

Part Two: Test Your Skills

DIRECTIONS: *Each group of sentences below has a cause and two effects. Place the correct letters in the spaces provided (C for Cause, E for Effect) to show which statement is the cause and which statements are the effects.*

15. _____ Northwest Coast Indians learned how to build canoes.

_____ Northwest Coast Indians lived along the Pacific Ocean.

_____ Northwest Coast Indians got most of their food from the sea.

16. _____ The Hopis filled a part of their homes with jars of corn and flour.

_____ The Hopis used water from underground to water their crops.

_____ The Hopis lived in an arid climate.

17. _____ Plains Indians hunted buffalo by following the buffalo herds.

_____ Plains Indians needed a source of food.

_____ Plains Indians made tepees that could be put up and taken down easily when the Indians hunted.

18. _____ The Aztecs built canals and paved roads to connect the islands in Lake Texcoco to the shore.

_____ The Aztecs needed more land for farming.

_____ The Aztecs built small islands in Lake Texcoco.

(continued)

Part Three: Apply What You Have Learned

DIRECTIONS: *Complete each of the following activities.*

19. *Indian Homes*

Match the descriptions of the Indian homes on the left with the names on the right. The names of the Indian groups that built the homes are in parentheses.

_____ a house built partly over a hole dug
in the ground

      A. pueblo (Hopi)

_____ a house made of elm bark with large doors
at each end; home for several families

      B. hogan (Navajo)

_____ a cone-shaped house made of a log frame
covered by mud or grass

      C. pit house
         (Chinook)

_____ an adobe building with rooms on top of and
next to one another; home for many families

      D. longhouse
         (Iroquois)

_____ a cone-shaped house made of poles and
covered with buffalo skins

      E. tepee
         (Mandan)

20. *Essay*

Many of the early cultures and civilizations borrowed ideas or products of earlier peoples and made them better. The Mayas borrowed from the Olmecs, and the Navajos borrowed from the Hopis. Choose either the Mayas or the Navajos and tell what ideas or products they borrowed from earlier peoples.

Unit 1 Test

Part One: Test Your Understanding

DIRECTIONS: *Circle the letter of the best answer.*

1. The land bridge that once linked Asia and North America is called
    A. Adenas.
    B. Siberia.
    C. Beringia.
    D. Central America.

2. Which of these is used by Indian peoples to explain their beliefs about the world and their place in it?
    A. potlatches
    B. longhouses
    C. confederations
    D. origin stories

3. Each native group that settled in the Americas developed its own way of life, or
    A. kachina.
    B. legend.
    C. diversity.
    D. culture.

4. Which of these sentences about Clovis points is correct?
    A. Clovis points were used to make fires.
    B. Clovis points made hunting easier.
    C. A spear with a Clovis point could be thrown farther.
    D. Clovis points were useful in making pottery.

5. Making baskets, living in winter and summer camps, and hunting small animals such as deer, rabbit, and antelope are changes that took place
    A. before the land bridge linking Asia and North America was covered with water.
    B. before the atlatl was invented.
    C. while people lived near glaciers.
    D. after the giant Ice-Age mammals became extinct.

(continued)

6. The most important crop grown in the Americas was
    A. corn.   **B.** wheat.
    C. squash.   **D.** beans.

7. The earthworks built by the Mound Builders were probably used for
    A. weapons.   **B.** agricultural fields.
    C. campgrounds.   **D.** religious purposes.

8. Early peoples exchanged ideas and products through
    A. specialization.   **B.** technology.
    C. trade.   **D.** shamans.

9. During a potlatch the Indians of the Northwest would
    A. give away gifts as a sign of their wealth.
    B. build pit houses for all the clan members.
    C. sing to a whale just before killing it.
    D. carve the history of their families on wooden posts.

10. How did the Hopis prepare for the possibility of drought?
    A. They built pueblos.
    B. They built large lakes to store water.
    C. They built special houses in the mountains.
    D. They stored surplus food.

11. Which of the following activities did the Navajos learn from the Hopis?
    A. hunting and gathering
    B. growing crops and weaving
    C. building canoes and houses
    D. making adobe and totem poles

12. What is the name for an adobe building that has many rooms built on top of and next to one another?
    A. hogan   **B.** pueblo
    C. pit house   **D.** kiva

(continued)

13. The Mandans made their shelters, moccasins, arrowheads, and blankets from
    A. the crops they grew.
    B. the fish they caught.
    C. the buffalo they hunted.
    D. the beavers they trapped.

14. The Iroquois formed a confederation because they wanted to
    A. move to the Northwest.
    B. develop a common trading language.
    C. build larger pueblos.
    D. put an end to the fighting among Indian tribes.

15. The Cherokees used plants in the forests for
    A. medicine.   **B.** fishing.
    C. money.   **D.** gifts.

16. The Mayas developed their civilization by borrowing and building on the ideas and achievements of the
    A. Hopis.   **B.** Aztecs.
    C. Cherokees.   **D.** Olmecs.

17. Which of the following was created by the Aztecs?
    A. tribe   **B.** clan
    C. city-state   **D.** empire

(continued)

Part Two: *Test Your Skills*

DIRECTIONS: Use the map below to answer the following questions.

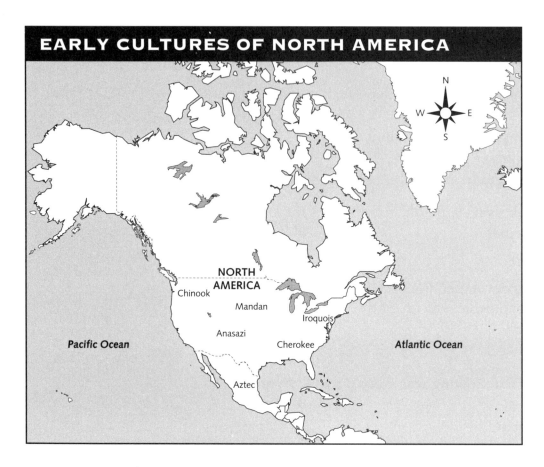

EARLY CULTURES OF NORTH AMERICA

18. The Anasazi lived in which direction from the Chinooks? _____

19. In which direction would a group of Iroquois travel to visit a

Cherokee tribe? _____

20. Which tribe shown on this map lived the farthest south? _____

(continued)

Part Three: Apply What You Have Learned

DIRECTIONS: *Complete each of the following activities.*

21. **Indian Peoples and Technology**
Technology is the use of scientific knowledge or tools to make or do something. In the following list, circle two items that are examples of technology. Then on the lines below, explain why they are examples of technology.

legend	theory	buffalo hide	atlatl
tribe	mesa	Clovis point	clan

_____

_____

22. **Essay**
Water is an important resource for all peoples and can affect a people's way of life. Write one paragraph telling how water affected the Indian peoples of the Northwest Coast and one paragraph telling how it affected the Indian peoples of the Southwest.

Individual Performance Task
History Comic Strips

Comic strips have been included in daily newspapers for more than a hundred years, and comic books have been around for more than sixty years. Comic books and comic strips have focused on many subjects and themes.

A newspaper comic strip usually has
- a story or part of a story told in four scenes or "boxes."
- captions in some of the boxes, either above or below the scenes, that explain what is happening.
- "word balloons" that tell what the people in the scene are saying. Each word balloon points to the person who is speaking.

Create a four-box history comic strip about one of the peoples you read about in Chapter 1 or Chapter 2. In the comic strip, show how these people worked together to solve their problems or reach their goals. Give your comic strip a title that goes with the cooperative activity the people are doing.

Group Performance Task
Panel Discussion

All human activity is affected by the environments in which people live. The peoples you studied in Chapters 1 and 2 lived in many different environments. As a result, they had different lifeways.

In a panel discussion, two or more people will make presentations to the class. The people on the panel will speak about the same subject, but each will cover a different part of the subject.

In this activity the class will be divided into groups of four students. Each group will then choose a people studied in this unit and present a panel discussion about them to the class. Each panel discussion should last between 10 and 15 minutes. During the panel discussion, each person on the panel will cover one of the following topics:
- a description of the environment in which the people lived
- how the environment affected the kind of food they ate
- how the environment affected the kind of transportation they used
- how the environment affected the kind of housing they lived in

Each person on the panel should use the textbook or other resources to gather information for his or her part of the panel discussion. Panel members should each make one visual aid (chart or picture) that they can use to help explain their topic. One student should be chosen as the panel moderator. The moderator will introduce the subject of the discussion and will introduce each panel member before he or she speaks.

In planning a panel discussion (or any oral report), keep these things in mind:
- Know your information so you can tell it in your own words.
- Speak slowly and clearly so everyone can hear you.
- Look at your audience.
- Respect your classmates. Be a good listener when they are presenting their panel discussions.

NAME _____ DATE _____

Chapter Test 3

Part One: Test Your Understanding

DIRECTIONS: *Match the descriptions on the left with the names on the right. Then write the correct letter in the space provided.*

_____ **1.** first European people known to have visited the Americas

_____ **2.** leader of first Europeans to visit the Americas

_____ **3.** name of the first European settlement in the Americas

_____ **4.** first European to make a globe

_____ **5.** European whose descriptions of the riches of China made traders want to go to Asia

_____ **6.** city captured by the Turks, closing off trade routes between Europe and Asia

_____ **7.** Portuguese leader who started a school for navigators

_____ **8.** Portuguese explorer who was the first European to sail around the southern tip of Africa

_____ **9.** Portuguese explorer who found a sea route to Asia by sailing around Africa

_____ **10.** local name for the island on which Columbus first landed

_____ **11.** Italian explorer who landed in present-day Newfoundland but told people he had found Cathay

_____ **12.** Italian explorer who figured out that Columbus had not reached Asia

_____ **13.** body of water reached by Spanish explorer Vasco Núñez de Balboa

_____ **14.** European who proved it was possible to reach Asia by sailing west from Europe

A. Prince Henry

B. Giovanni Caboto

C. Ferdinand Magellan

D. Leif Eriksson

E. Pacific Ocean

F. Constantinople

G. Vikings

H. Vinland

I. Vasco da Gama

J. Martin Behaim

K. Amerigo Vespucci

L. Guanahani

M. Marco Polo

N. Bartholomeu Dias

(continued)

NAME _____ DATE _____

Part Two: Test Your Skills

DIRECTIONS: Read the problem below. Then use the information in Statements
A through D to help you draw a conclusion that will answer the question in the box.
Write your conclusion on the lines below, and tell how you reached that conclusion.
Then list the letters of the statements that support your conclusion.

> **PROBLEM**—How could early explorers be sure that the
> Pacific Ocean and the Atlantic Ocean were two different
> bodies of water?

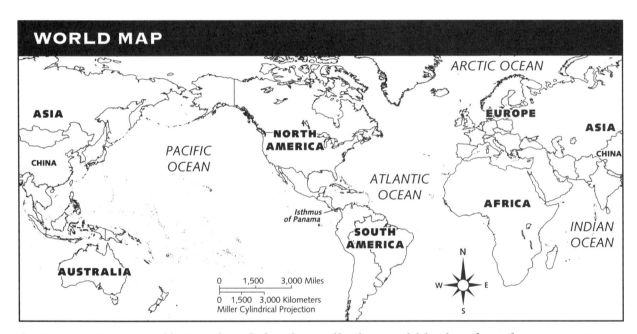

WORLD MAP

Statement A: Christopher Columbus tells the world he has found a new water
route to Asia by sailing west from Europe. (1492)

Statement B: Giovanni Caboto announces he has sailed west from Europe to
China. (1497)

Statement C: Vasco Núñez de Balboa crosses the Isthmus of Panama. (1513)

Statement D: Ferdinand Magellan sails his ship around the southern tip of South
America. (1520)

15. Conclusion: _____

_____

_____

16. Statements that support your conclusion: _____

(continued)

Part Three: Apply What You Have Learned

DIRECTIONS: *Complete each of the following activities.*

17. *Changes in Europe*

By the time the trade routes between Europe and Asia had been closed off, many changes had taken place in Europe. In the box below, list three changes in technology and one change in government that helped set the stage for European exploration.

TECHNOLOGY	GOVERNMENT
1. _____ _____	1. _____ _____
2. _____ _____	_____ _____
3. _____ _____	_____ _____

18. *A Sequence of Events*

The story of European exploration follows a sequence of events. Place the following events in their proper sequence by numbering them from 1 to 6, with 1 being the earliest event and 6 being the latest event.

_____ The first European school for training sailors in navigation is set up.

_____ One of Ferdinand Magellan's ships sails around the world.

_____ Amerigo Vespucci concludes that Columbus did not reach Asia.

_____ Christopher Columbus receives support from Spain to sail to Asia.

_____ The trade routes between Europe and Asia are closed off.

_____ Vasco Núñez de Balboa proves that Vespucci was right and that Columbus was wrong.

(continued)

19. *Essay*

The first globe ever made in Europe was created by a German mapmaker who lived in Nuremberg, Germany. Although the globe was a remarkable creation, it had many things wrong with it. Write one paragraph explaining what was wrong with the globe.

Chapter Test 4

Part One: Test Your Understanding

DIRECTIONS: *Match the descriptions on the left with the names on the right. Then write the correct letter in the space provided.*

_____ 1. Aztec leader when Europeans came to Mexico

_____ 2. leader of the Spanish conquistadors who conquered the Aztecs

_____ 3. Spanish conquistador who ordered his soldiers to kill the Inca emperor

_____ 4. leader of Incas killed by the Spanish

_____ 5. Spanish explorer who looked for the Fountain of Youth and named present-day Florida

_____ 6. Spanish explorer who heard stories about the Seven Cities of Gold and set out to find them

_____ 7. explorer who claimed for Spain all of what is today the southeastern United States

_____ 8. people who came to the Americas to convert native peoples to Christianity

_____ 9. peoples brought to the Americas against their will and forced to work for the colonists

_____ 10. explorer who looked for the Northwest Passage

_____ 11. explorer who founded Quebec and Montreal

_____ 12. European who founded a colony at Roanoke Island that soon disappeared

_____ 13. peoples who died from hunger, overwork, and diseases after being enslaved by the Spanish

_____ 14. Indian who taught the Pilgrims how to fish and plant crops that would do well

A. Africans

B. Atahuallpa

C. Motecuhzoma

D. Tisquantum

E. Francisco Pizarro

F. Sir Walter Raleigh

G. Hernando de Soto

H. Samuel de Champlain

I. Hernando Cortés

J. Indian peoples

K. Jacques Cartier

L. Juan Ponce de León

M. missionaries

N. Francisco Vásquez de Coronado

(continued)

Part Two: Test Your Skills

DIRECTIONS: *Use the information in the time line to answer the following questions.*

15. Which colony started first—Roanoke or St. Augustine?

_____

16. How many years after Magellan's ship returned home did Drake sail around the world?

_____

17. When did Hernando de Soto reach the Mississippi River?

_____

18. Which was started later—Plymouth or New Amsterdam?

_____

19. When was the Plymouth colony founded? How many years was this after Elizabeth I became queen?

_____

20. Where was the first English colony in North America? How many years was it until a second colony was set up by the English in North America?

_____

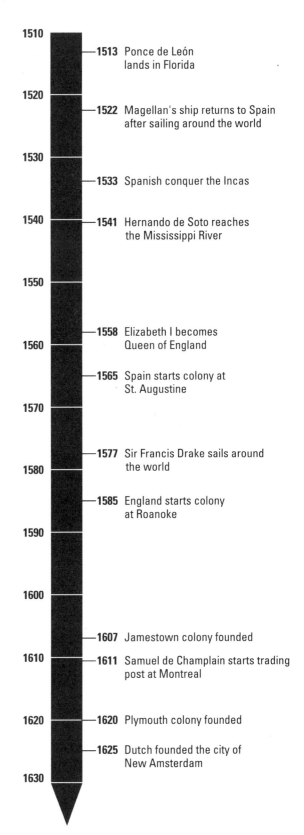

1510

—**1513** Ponce de León lands in Florida

1520

—**1522** Magellan's ship returns to Spain after sailing around the world

1530

—**1533** Spanish conquer the Incas

1540 —**1541** Hernando de Soto reaches the Mississippi River

1550

—**1558** Elizabeth I becomes Queen of England

1560

—**1565** Spain starts colony at St. Augustine

1570

—**1577** Sir Francis Drake sails around the world

1580

—**1585** England starts colony at Roanoke

1590

1600

—**1607** Jamestown colony founded

1610 —**1611** Samuel de Champlain starts trading post at Montreal

1620 —**1620** Plymouth colony founded

—**1625** Dutch founded the city of New Amsterdam

1630

(continued)

Part Three: Apply What You Have Learned

DIRECTIONS: *Complete each of the following activities.*

21. *Colonial Empires*

The colonies founded by Europeans in the Americas produced great wealth. In the chart below, list the areas where European countries had colonies and the source of profit for each country.

COUNTRY	AREA	SOURCE OF WEALTH
Spain		
Holland		
France		
England		

(continued)

22. *Reasons for Coming to America*

Europeans had many reasons for setting up colonies in the Americas. Write in the chart the goal of each group listed.

GROUP	GOAL
French government	
Virginia Company	
Pilgrims	

23. *Essay*

There was both cooperation and conflict between the colonists and the Native Americans. Write one paragraph discussing ways in which colonists and Indians cooperated and one paragraph discussing ways in which they were in conflict.

Unit 2 Test

Part One: Test Your Understanding

DIRECTIONS: *Circle the letter of the best answer.*

1. The Viking settlement of Vinland was located in present-day
    A. Iceland.   **B.** United States.
    C. Canada.   **D.** Greenland.

2. One of the major problems with the globe made by Martin Behaim was that
    A. there was no north direction.
    B. the Atlantic Ocean was missing.
    C. there were continents missing.
    D. there were no longitude and latitude.

3. Marco Polo returned to Europe with stories about the riches of
    A. China.   **B.** Plymouth.
    C. Vinland.   **D.** Guanahani.

4. Europeans were eager to trade with Asia because they wanted
    A. silk, spices, and gold.
    B. wood, seashells, and silver.
    C. clocks, mirrors, and beads.
    D. vegetables, spices, and fruit.

5. Trade between Europe and Asia was stopped when the Turks captured
    A. Roanoke.   **B.** Damascus.
    C. Rome.   **D.** Constantinople.

6. Amerigo Vespucci used information he gathered from his voyages to conclude that
    A. the Northwest Passage did not exist.
    B. the Aztecs controlled the Seven Cities of Gold.
    C. Christopher Columbus had not reached Asia.
    D. the Vikings had not reached the Americas.

7. The explorer whose ship was the first to sail around the world was
    A. Vasco Núñez de Balboa.
    B. Ferdinand Magellan.
    C. Christopher Columbus.
    D. Juan Ponce de León.

(continued)

8. It was easy for Cortés and his soldiers to conquer the Aztecs because
    A. the Aztecs had fought a civil war and were very weak.
    B. the Aztec leaders could not be trusted.
    C. the Aztecs lived in a land that had no physical barriers.
    D. the Aztecs did not have guns or cannons.

9. The Spanish were able to conquer the Incas because
    A. a strong earthquake destroyed the main Inca cities.
    B. the Incas thought Pizarro was a god.
    C. the Spanish killed Atahuallpa, the Inca leader.
    D. the Incas had fewer soldiers than the Spanish.

10. The Spanish word for "conqueror" is
    A. cartographer.   **B.** monarch.
    C. conquistador.   **D.** navigator.

11. The Virginia Company of London sent colonists to Jamestown to
    A. build a trading post.
    B. work in the mines.
    C. conquer the Olmecs.
    D. find the Northwest Passage.

12. The main result of the fighting between the Hurons and the Iroquois for control of the fur trade was that
    A. the supply of furs grew smaller and smaller.
    B. the Europeans gained control of Indian land.
    C. the Dutch were forced out of their colony of New Amsterdam.
    D. they joined together to take control of the fur trade.

13. The idea of "no work, no food" as it applied to the Jamestown colony was stated by
    A. John Smith.   **B.** Queen Elizabeth I.
    C. Sir Walter Raleigh.   **D.** John Rolfe.

14. The main reason the Pilgrims came to the Americas was
    A. to find gold and silver.
    B. to gain religious freedom.
    C. to set up colonies for the French government.
    D. to take control of the fur trade.

(continued)

NAME _____ DATE _____

Part Two: Test Your Skills

DIRECTIONS: *Use the map of South Carolina to answer the following questions.*

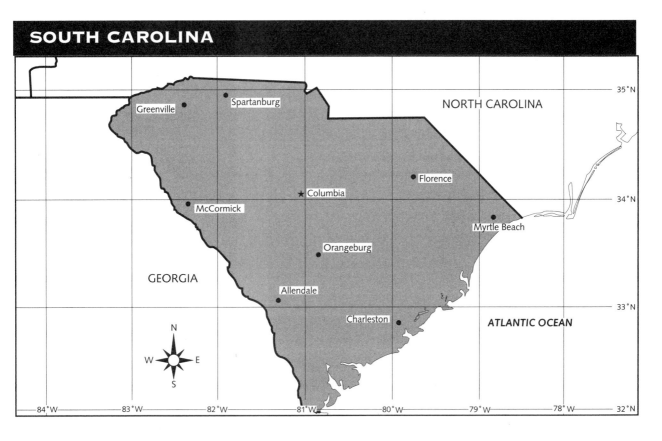

15. What line of latitude is closest to Florence? _____

16. What line of longitude is closest to Orangeburg? _____

17. What city is located near 33°N, 81°W? _____

18. What city is located near 35°N, 82°W? _____

19. What is the latitude and longitude for Columbia, South Carolina?

_____

20. Which city is closer to 83°W—Spartanburg or Greenville? _____

(continued)

Part Three: Apply What You Have Learned

DIRECTIONS: *Complete each of the following activities.*

21. *Spanish Colonies and Labor*

The Spanish were able to gain control over large areas in the islands and on the mainland in the Americas. One of the first problems they faced was finding people to do the work in their new empire. Fill in the chart below about who did the work for the Spanish and how these people were treated.

What group of people did the Spanish first use as slaves to work on their plantations and in their mines?

_____

_____

_____

How were these people treated?

_____

_____

_____

What was the second group of people the Spanish used as slaves to work on their plantations and in their mines?

_____

_____

_____

How were these people treated?

_____

_____

_____

(continued)

22. *The Mayflower Compact*

The Mayflower Compact was an important document in the history of the United States. Fill in the information about this document in the chart.

THE MAYFLOWER COMPACT	
What was this document?	
Why was it written?	
Why is it important?	

23. *Essay*

Changes in Europe helped set the stage for European exploration. Write one paragraph discussing the changes in technology that encouraged Europeans to try to find a new route to Asia.

Individual Performance Task
A Traveler in the Americas

Marco Polo was 17 years old when he went with his father to China. When he came back 24 years later, he told many stories about what he had seen during his travels in China and all through Asia. Few people believed him when he told of his adventures.

Imagine that you are a world traveler like Marco Polo and you have visited the Americas. Your task is to write a story for your friends back in Europe about what you have seen in the Americas. Follow these steps in writing your story:

Step 1 Choose one of the following places to visit:
- Vinland
- Peru
- Plymouth
- the Caribbean
- Florida
- Mexico
- Jamestown

Step 2 Reread the section in the text that discusses the place you have chosen. You may also want to read other materials to gather more information about the place.

Step 3 Make an outline of the information you will include in your story. You may want to cover:
- animal life
- geography
- people (clothing, housing, language)
- climate
- natural resources
- farming
- tools and weapons

Step 4 Write a rough draft of your story. Review and revise your rough draft to be sure it has all the information you want to present.

Step 5 Have a classmate read your rough draft. Ask your classmate if anything is unclear or confusing.

Step 6 Revise and edit your draft, and make a final copy.

Group Performance Task
Make an Encounter Mural

Create a mural showing an encounter that took place when a European or a group of Europeans arrived in an area of the world new to them. You may use one of the encounters listed below for your mural, or you may wish to choose a different encounter.

- Marco Polo meets Kublai Khan.
- Christopher Columbus meets the people of Guanahani.
- Cortés meets Motecuhzoma.
- John Smith meets Pocahontas.
- Pilgrims meet Tisquantum.

Form a group with three or four of your classmates, and then follow these steps in making your mural:

Step 1 Choose an encounter and research it. Use the materials in the textbook as well as materials in the library. Make sure that your mural shows only what really happened.

Step 2 After you have done your research, choose a title for your mural and decide what will go into it. Be sure to create some written material to put next to your mural to explain to viewers what the mural is about.

Step 3 Make sketches in pencil on the mural paper. Then use paints, crayons, and markers to complete your mural.

Chapter 5 Test

Part One: Test Your Understanding

DIRECTIONS: *Circle the letter of the best answer.*

1. The Spanish government created the Spanish borderlands north of New Spain to
   A. establish an Indian farming area.
   B. make room for the horses brought from Spain.
   C. protect its gold and silver mines.
   D. protect its fur trade.

2. The Spanish built presidios to
   A. protect their navy.
   B. teach the Indians about Christianity.
   C. encourage cattle and sheep raising.
   D. protect settlers.

3. The oldest permanent European settlement in the United States is
   A. St. Augustine.   B. Jamestown.
   C. Plymouth.   D. New Orleans.

4. How did Spanish settlements in the borderlands change the lives of the Indians living there?
   A. The Indians learned how to farm.
   B. The Indians began to create origin stories.
   C. The Indians learned how to tame horses and raise sheep.
   D. The Indians began to build haciendas.

5. Life was hard for the Indians who lived at the Spanish missions because
   A. the Spanish refused to protect them from their enemies.
   B. they had to leave their families and friends.
   C. they had to give up their religious traditions.
   D. the Spanish would not give them any work to do.

6. Why did King Louis XIV make New France a royal colony?
   A. He wanted to rebuild his hold in North America after the fur trade was nearly destroyed.
   B. He wanted to force the Spanish to remove their presidios from New France.
   C. He wanted to raise taxes.
   D. He wanted to move to Montreal.

(continued)

7. When Jacques Marquette and Louis Joliet went looking for the Mississippi River, they hoped the river would help them find
   A. New Amsterdam.
   B. the Fountain of Youth.
   C. the Seven Cities of Gold.
   D. a route to Asia.

8. Who claimed the area known as Louisiana for the French?
   A. King Charles I
   B. William Penn
   C. Sieur de La Salle
   D. Count de Frontenac

9. In a proprietary colony the ownership belongs to
   A. the king.
   B. a company.
   C. one person.
   D. the settlers.

10. Which of these best explains why the Virginia Company of London founded the Jamestown colony?
   A. It was to be a trading post to make a profit for the company.
   B. It was to be a port for whaling ships.
   C. It was to be the first colony in California.
   D. It was to bring Christianity to the Indian tribes living in the area.

11. The most important cash crop in Virginia and Maryland was
   A. rice.   B. wheat.
   C. indigo.   D. tobacco.

12. The Puritans founded their colony in Massachusetts to
   A. search for gold.   B. make a profit from fishing.
   C. sell furs to New France. D. practice their religion.

13. The Connecticut colony adopted the Fundamental Orders, which was
   A. the first written system of government in North America.
   B. a set of guidelines for setting up the first school in North America.
   C. a promise to obey the orders of the British king.
   D. a plan to distribute indigo seeds to the other British colonies.

14. William Penn established Pennsylvania as a refuge for
   A. Indian peoples.   B. Jews.
   C. Catholics.   D. Quakers.

(continued)

Part Two: Test Your Skills

DIRECTIONS: Use the information in the table to classify the colonies in three different ways. You may use abbreviations for the colonies when you write them in the charts below.

THE BRITISH COLONIES			
COLONY	DATE STARTED	TYPE OF GOVERNMENT	POPULATION (1770)
Connecticut (CT)	1635	Self-governing	183,881
Delaware (DE)	1638	Controlled by an owner	35,496
Georgia (GA)	1733	Controlled by the king	23,375
Maryland (MD)	1634	Controlled by an owner	202,612
Massachusetts (MA)	1620	Controlled by the king	235,308
New Hampshire (NH)	1623	Controlled by the king	62,396
New Jersey (NJ)	1664	Controlled by the king	117,431
New York (NY)	1613	Controlled by the king	162,920
North Carolina (NC)	1653	Controlled by the king	197,200
Pennsylvania (PA)	1681	Controlled by an owner	240,657
Rhode Island (RI)	1636	Self-governing	58,196
South Carolina (SC)	1670	Controlled by the king	124,244
Virginia (VA)	1607	Controlled by the king	447,016

DATE STARTED	
COLONIES STARTED BEFORE 1650	COLONIES STARTED AFTER 1650
15.	16.

TYPE OF GOVERNMENT		
CONTROLLED BY THE KING	CONTROLLED BY AN OWNER	SELF-GOVERNING
17.	18.	19.

POPULATION	
LESS THAN 100,000	MORE THAN 200,000
20.	21.

(continued)

Part Three: Apply What You Have Learned

DIRECTIONS: *Complete each of the following activities.*

22. **European Colonies in North America**

    Spain, France, and England all built colonial empires in North America. Listed below are six items that relate to these empires. Put each item in the proper column, and write a short description of each. The first one has been done for you.

    - El Camino Real
    - charter
    - James Oglethorpe
    - John Law
    - portage
    - St. Augustine

SPAIN	FRANCE	ENGLAND
El Camino Real "the Royal Road" linked missions and presidios in the borderlands c. _____	a. _____ d. _____	b. _____ e. _____

23. **Essay**

    There were no plantations in Georgia before 1750. Explain why this was so, and explain why this changed after 1750.

Chapter Test 6

Part One: Test Your Understanding

DIRECTIONS: *Circle the letter of the best answer.*

1. In most New England towns, the meetinghouse was used both
   A. as a jail and as a place of government.
   B. as a house of worship and as a place of government.
   C. as a house of worship and as a general store.
   D. as a general store and as a jail.

2. What was the purpose of a town meeting?
   A. to collect taxes for the king
   B. to educate boys and girls
   C. to have people work together to build wagons
   D. to make decisions about laws and town workers

3. How did market towns help farmers who lived near them?
   A. Market towns were a place where women, Africans, and Native
      Americans could vote.
   B. Farmers could trade their crops for goods and services.
   C. Every market town had a college where people could finish their education.
   D. British brokers visited these towns to buy tobacco.

4. The triangular trade route linked
   A. Britain, British colonies, and Africa.
   B. market towns, county seats, and plantations.
   C. British colonies, Asia, and Africa.
   D. colonial cities, market towns, and plantations.

5. Which of these economic activities contributed to the growth of cities along the
   Atlantic coast?
   A. whaling   B. dairy farming
   C. growing tobacco   D. growing indigo

6. Young people who lived in cities learned to do jobs that required special skills by
   A. going to college.   B. becoming apprentices.
   C. traveling in Conestoga wagons.   D. following the triangular trade route.

(continued)

7. In the southern colonies, most of the land was owned by
    A. brokers.
    B. church officials.
    C. planters.
    D. small farmers.

8. Early southern plantations were usually built
    A. along waterways.
    B. in cities.
    C. along major roads.
    D. near mountains.

9. What did southern plantation owners use instead of money?
    A. fish
    B. furs
    C. crops
    D. gold

10. Planters most often sold their farm products through
    A. British brokers.
    B. indentured servants.
    C. apprentices.
    D. constables.

11. Indentured servants
    A. were in charge of trade in the cities.
    B. always went willingly to the colonies.
    C. had to work for a set period of time without pay.
    D. agreed to work for a lifetime in trade for their children's freedom.

12. Wealthy planters were able to do the work required on large plantations with the help of
    A. British brokers.
    B. enslaved Native Americans.
    C. the local militia.
    D. enslaved Africans.

13. Which of the following best describes the education received by the daughters of southern planters?
    A. They learned science and math.
    B. They learned to read and sew.
    C. They went to college in Britain.
    D. They received no education.

14. The land between the Coastal Plain and the Appalachian Mountains is known as the
    A. heartland.
    B. fall line.
    C. backcountry.
    D. prairie.

15. Travel on the Great Wagon Road
    A. was very easy.
    B. was the only way to get wagons to the ocean.
    C. was important to the settlement of the backcountry.
    D. was one of the many roads that led to the backcountry.

(continued)

NAME _____ DATE _____

Part Two: Test Your Skills

DIRECTIONS: *Use the information on the product map to answer the following questions.*

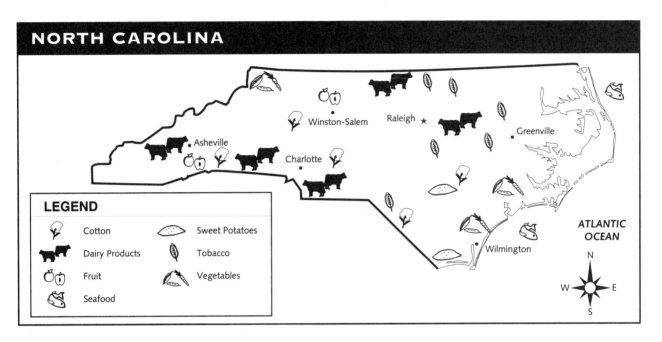

16. In what part of North Carolina would you find sweet potatoes as the major crop?

_____

17. What is produced near Asheville? _____

18. How can you tell that tobacco is the main farm product in North Carolina?

_____

19. In which North Carolina city would you find businesses involved with fishing and

seafood? _____

20. What is produced near Charlotte, North Carolina? _____

_____

(continued)

Part Three: Apply What You Have Learned

DIRECTIONS: *Complete each of the following activities.*

21. **Water Transportation**
    Transportation by water was very important in the British colonies. Listed below are five terms that are connected to water transportation. Explain how each term is related to water transportation.

    a. indentured servants _____

    _____

    b. raw materials _____

    c. slaves _____

    d. tobacco _____

    e. whale products _____

    _____

22. **Exports and Imports**
    Exports and imports were an important part of the economies of the British colonies. In the chart below, list five exports and five imports of the British colonies.

EXPORTS	IMPORTS
a.	f.
b.	g.
c.	h.
d.	i.
e.	j.

23. **Essay**
    The running of a plantation required the participation of all the people living there. Write one paragraph about the jobs of the planter and the planter's wife.

Unit 3 Test

Part One: Test Your Understanding

DIRECTIONS: Circle the letter of the best answer.

1. St. Augustine was
   A. the main American port in the triangular trade route.
   B. the most important French mission in the British colonies.
   C. the main whaling port in New England.
   D. the first permanent European settlement in what is now the United States.

2. The Spanish government built roads linking Spanish missions to
   A. presidios.   **B.** whaling centers.
   C. southern plantations.   **D.** haciendas.

3. Which French explorers were convinced that they had found La Salle's river?
   A. Marquette and Joliet   **B.** Cartier and Frontenac
   C. Iberville and Bienville   **D.** Mongoulacha and Louisville

4. Which of these colonies was **not** founded for religious reasons?
   A. Plymouth   **B.** Jamestown
   C. Massachusetts   **D.** Maryland

5. Which of these areas in North America was made a proprietary colony by the king of France?
   A. Ontario   **B.** Quebec
   C. Louisiana   **D.** Florida

6. The town of Strawberry Banke, later to become the colony of New Hampshire, was started as
   A. a place to grow strawberries.
   B. a major trading post.
   C. a refuge for Quakers.
   D. a place to cut and ship lumber.

7. Decisions about the government in many New England towns were made by
   A. militias.
   B. proprietors.
   C. citizens at town meetings.
   D. British brokers.

(continued)

DIRECTIONS: *Match the descriptions on the left with the words on the right. Write the correct letter in the space provided.*

_____ **8.** a military fort built for the protection of settlers in the Spanish borderlands

_____ **9.** a small community of Catholic religious workers in the Spanish colonies

A. broker

_____ **10.** a person who has been in prison for owing money

B. presidio

C. militia

_____ **11.** a town's voluntary army

D. indentured servant

_____ **12.** a person who worked without pay to pay the cost of coming to the Americas

E. mission

F. auction

_____ **13.** a person paid to buy and sell things for someone else

G. debtor

H. fall line

_____ **14.** a place where slaves were bought and sold

_____ **15.** a place where the land drops sharply, causing rivers to form waterfalls

(continued)

Part Two: Test Your Skills

DIRECTIONS: *The information in the circle graphs shows exports and imports in the British colonies. The graph on the left shows where the exports of the colonies came from. The graph on the right shows where the imports went. Use the information in the graphs and what you know from reading the unit to answer the following questions.*

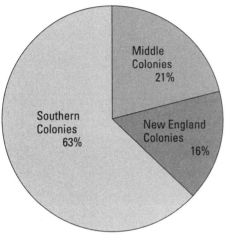

Exports, 1772

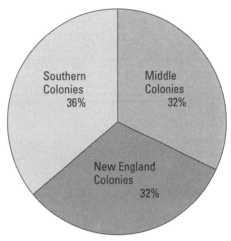

Imports, 1772

16. Which colonies had the most exports? What was the major product that was exported from these colonies?

_____

17. What percent of the exports came from the middle colonies? Why do you think these colonies had fewer exports than the southern colonies?

_____

_____

18. Which colonies had the most imports? Why do you think these colonies imported the most?

_____

_____

_____

(continued)

Part Three: Apply What You Have Learned

DIRECTIONS: *Complete each of the following activities.*

19. *Triangular Trade Route*

The triangular trade route was important to the economy of Britain and the British colonies. On the map below, draw the triangular trade route. On each side of the triangle, write the items that were carried by the ships on that part of the route.

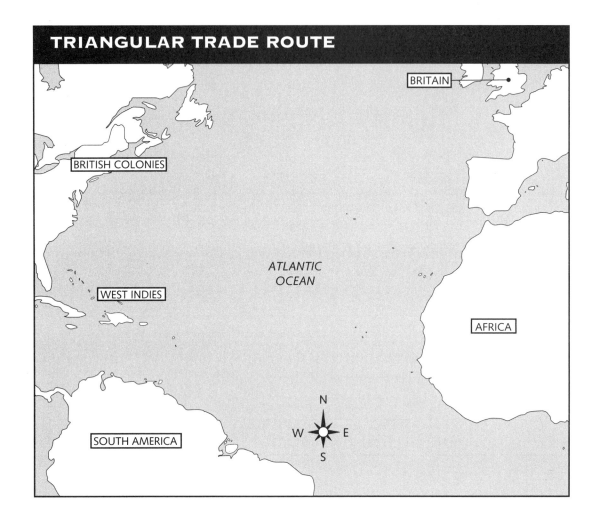

(continued)

NAME _____ DATE _____

20. *Essay*

The middle colonies attracted a wide diversity of European immigrants. Write a paragraph explaining why such a variety of people moved to the middle colonies.

Individual Performance Task

Imports and Exports

Trade was an important economic activity in the British colonies of North America. Listed below are some figures that show the value of imports and exports. Use the figures to make a bar graph. Your bar graph should show the value of both imports and exports from 1700 through 1750. The graph must have a title and labels.

After you finish making your bar graph, compare the values of imports with the values of exports. Write a list of trends you can see or conclusions you can make from your graph.

EXPORTS FROM NEW YORK TO BRITAIN AND IMPORTS TO NEW YORK FROM BRITAIN 1700–1750		
All figures are rounded to the nearest thousand. All amounts are given in pounds sterling. (The British unit of currency is the pound sterling.)		
Date	Imports	Exports
1700	49,000	18,000
1710	31,000	8,000
1720	37,000	17,000
1730	64,000	9,000
1740	119,000	21,000
1750	267,000	36,000

Group Performance Task
A Radio Commercial

There was always a need for people to work in the British colonies in America. One way people in the colonies met their labor needs was by hiring indentured servants. Colonists would pay the cost of a worker's trip to America. In return, the person would work for that colonist for a set period of time without pay.

In this activity, the class will be divided into groups of five students each. Each group will create a radio commercial that would attract people in Britain to come to America as indentured servants. (Imagine that radio had been invented during the colonial period.)

In planning your radio commercial, keep these things in mind:

- The commercial should be 90 seconds long and should be recorded on an audiocassette.
- There must be a written script for the commercial.
- There must be at least five people in the commercial. You will need an announcer, a plantation owner, the wife of the plantation owner, a male indentured servant, and a female indentured servant.
- The commercial should give information about the benefits of coming to the colonies, the type of work to be done, and the number of years the person must work as an indentured servant. It should also describe the climate, food, recreational activities, and lifeways in the colony.
- The commercial can use background music and sound effects. You should be as creative as possible while remaining true to history.

Chapter Test 7

Part One: Test Your Understanding

DIRECTIONS: *Fill in the blank with the correct word or name from the list below.*

Boston Tea Party	boycott	buyout
Committees of Correspondence	Concord	Crispus Attucks
French Canada	House of Burgesses	Loyalists
Minutemen	Parliament	quarter
repealed	representation	Sons of Liberty
tariff	taxes	

1. The British _____ made laws for all British people.

2. The first colonial legislature, called the _____, was started in the Virginia colony.

3. After the French and Indian War, _____ became a British colony.

4. American colonists were asked to pay for the cost of the French and Indian War by paying _____.

5. The Sugar Act angered many colonists because it required them to pay a _____, or tax, on goods brought into the colonies.

6. Colonists who supported the actions of the British government were known as Tories, or _____.

7. Many colonists were against the Stamp Act because it was an example of taxation without _____.

(continued)

8. Many colonists protested the Stamp Act with a _____ of British goods.

9. Parliament _____ the Stamp Act when it heard that nine of the colonies sent representatives to the Stamp Act Congress.

10. _____ was a runaway slave who was killed by British soldiers in the Boston Massacre.

11. The colonists formed the _____ to keep colonists informed about protests against British laws.

12. The Sons of Liberty protested the tax on tea with an action that later

became known as the _____.

13. Colonists in Massachusetts felt that to _____, or provide housing for, British soldiers was intolerable.

14. _____ were members of the Massachusetts militia who were always ready to defend the colony.

15. The fighting between the colonists and the British army that took place in

the towns of Lexington and _____ marked the beginning of the Revolutionary War.

(continued)

CHAPTER 7 TEST

Part Two: Test Your Skills

In the Spring of 1777, a soldier in the Continental army had an important decision to make. Should he continue to stay in the Continental army and serve with George Washington in the fight for American independence? Or should he return to his farm to plant crops so his family would have food for the next year?

In making his decision, this soldier had to determine the trade-offs (decide to do one thing and give up something else) and opportunity costs (what he would have to give up to get something else).

Fill in the chart below to explain the trade-offs and opportunity costs the soldier would have to consider to make his decision.

MAKING THE DECISION	
Trade-off in staying in the Continental army	**Trade-off in going home to plant crops**
16. a.	b.
Opportunity cost of staying in the Continental army	**Opportunity cost of going home to plant crops**
17. a.	b.

(continued)

Part Three: Apply What You Have Learned

DIRECTIONS: *Complete each of the following activities.*

18. *Actions and Reactions*

One action can lead to another. Listed below on the left are actions that happened in the colonies in the period before the Revolution. Fill in each box on the right with the reaction or reactions to that action.

ACTION	REACTION(S)
Britain wins the French and Indian War.	
The British government passes the Stamp Act.	
The British government passes a tax on tea brought into the colonies.	
The Sons of Liberty, disguised as Indians, dump British tea into Boston Harbor.	
British general hears that Patriot leaders and weapons are being hidden at Lexington and Concord.	

19. *Essay*

After the end of the French and Indian War, Britain passed the Proclamation of 1763. Write one paragraph explaining what the Proclamation of 1763 was, why it was passed, and how the colonists reacted to it.

Chapter 8 Test

Part One: Test Your Understanding

DIRECTIONS: *Match the descriptions on the left with the words or names on the right. Write the correct letters in the spaces provided.*

_____ **1.** meeting of colonial leaders to deal with the British reaction to Lexington and Concord

_____ **2.** letter sent by the Patriots to King George III, asking him to repeal the Intolerable Acts

_____ **3.** person chosen to lead the Continental army because of his understanding of soldiers

_____ **4.** soldiers hired by the British to help them in the Revolutionary War

_____ **5.** person who wrote *Common Sense* and urged the colonies to break away from Britain

_____ **6.** writer of the Declaration of Independence

_____ **7.** religious group whose members are pacifists and refuse to take part in war

_____ **8.** person who joined the North Carolina militia to fight at the Battle of Moores Creek

_____ **9.** person whose poems supported independence

_____ **10.** free African who fought at the Battle of Concord

_____ **11.** Polish officer who came to America to fight with the Continental army

_____ **12.** German soldier who helped train the Continental soldiers at Valley Forge

_____ **13.** American victory in the Revolutionary War that led France to help the Patriots

_____ **14.** battle that proved the Patriots had won the war

_____ **15.** agreement between the British and the Americans at the end of the Revolutionary War

A. Peter Salem

B. Second Continental Congress

C. Battle of Yorktown

D. Friedrich von Steuben

E. Treaty of Paris

F. mercenaries

G. Phillis Wheatley

H. Olive Branch Petition

I. George Washington

J. Battle of Saratoga

K. Thomas Jefferson

L. Mary Slocumb

M. Quakers

N. Thomas Paine

O. Thaddeus Kosciuszko

(continued)

Part Two: Test Your Skills

DIRECTIONS: *Use the information in the cartoon to answer the following questions.*

16. What is the man on the steps reading to the people? _____

_____

17. What choice must the people in the cartoon make? _____

_____

18. Why is this such an important choice for the people to make?

_____

_____

_____

(continued)

CHAPTER 8 TEST

Part Three: Apply What You Have Learned

DIRECTIONS: *Complete each of the following activities.*

19. *The Declaration of Independence*
The Declaration of Independence was very carefully planned and written. It remains one of the nation's most important documents. In the chart below, describe the purpose of each of the four parts of this document.

FIRST PART	SECOND PART	THIRD PART	FOURTH PART

(continued)

20. *Events in the Revolutionary War*
Place the following events in their proper sequence by numbering them from 1 to 6, with 1 being the earliest event and 6 being the latest event.

_____ American victory at the Battle of Yorktown

_____ Continental army spends the winter at Valley Forge, Pennsylvania

_____ Americans and British sign an agreement to end the war

_____ Americans fight the British at the Battle of Bunker Hill

_____ American victory over the British at the Battle of Saratoga

_____ Second Continental Congress declares independence

21. *Essay*
In the War for Independence, the British army had many advantages that the Continental army did not have. In a one-paragraph essay, compare and contrast the British army with the Continental army.

Unit 4 Test

Part One: Test Your Understanding

DIRECTIONS: *Circle the letter of the best answer.*

1. The laws for the colonies were made
- **A.** by the Continental army.
- **B.** by royal governors.
- **C.** by colonial legislatures.
- **D.** by colonial women.

2. Which of these was a result of the French and Indian War?
- **A.** The fur trade in North America stopped.
- **B.** The French took control of four more colonies.
- **C.** The Treaty of Paris was signed.
- **D.** Parliament decided the colonists should pay for part of the cost of the war.

3. Many colonists were angered by the Stamp Act because
- **A.** it was an example of taxation without representation.
- **B.** there were no post offices in the colonies.
- **C.** they were already paying for the tea that had been dumped into Boston Harbor.
- **D.** the Loyalists did not have to buy the stamps.

4. Crispus Attucks was
- **A.** the leader of the Stamp Act Congress.
- **B.** the first person killed at the Boston Massacre.
- **C.** a soldier who came from France to help the Continental army.
- **D.** the most important Loyalist leader in the colonies.

5. What was the purpose of the Committees of Correspondence?
- **A.** to punish the colonies because of the Boston Tea Party
- **B.** to persuade colonists to become Loyalists
- **C.** to pass news from colony to colony about protests against Britain
- **D.** to try to get Parliament to repeal the Stamp Act

6. Which of these events took place **last**?
- **A.** the meeting of the Continental Congress
- **B.** the Boston Massacre
- **C.** the Boston Tea Party
- **D.** protests against the Stamp Act

7. Who made George Washington the leader of the Continental army?
- **A.** the House of Burgesses
- **B.** the British Parliament
- **C.** the Minutemen
- **D.** the Second Continental Congress

(continued)

8. Which of these statements best describes the Continental army?
- **A.** Its soldiers were mercenary soldiers.
- **B.** Its soldiers were professional soldiers.
- **C.** Most of its soldiers signed up for a year and then went home.
- **D.** Most of its soldiers were well trained and had military experience.

9. *Common Sense,* a pamphlet urging the colonies to break away from Britain, was written by
- **A.** Benjamin Franklin.
- **B.** George Washington.
- **C.** Thomas Paine.
- **D.** George III.

10. Who wrote the Declaration of Independence?
- **A.** Benjamin Franklin
- **B.** George Washington
- **C.** Thomas Jefferson
- **D.** Thomas Paine

11. The writer of the Declaration of Independence included a list of the colonists' grievances in order to
- **A.** show the unfair things the king and Parliament had done.
- **B.** explain why the colonists were boycotting British tea.
- **C.** apologize to the British king for the actions of the Patriots.
- **D.** persuade Parliament to repeal the Stamp Act.

12. Which group of people refused to fight in the Revolutionary War because of their pacifist beliefs?
- **A.** Quakers
- **B.** Loyalists
- **C.** mercenaries
- **D.** Congregationalists

13. The enslaved Africans who enlisted in the Continental army
- **A.** taught the Continentals how to fight.
- **B.** supported the Loyalists.
- **C.** were promised freedom after the war.
- **D.** were all killed in the Boston Massacre.

14. The battle that convinced the French that the colonists could really defeat the British was
- **A.** the Battle of Lexington.
- **B.** the Battle of Yorktown.
- **C.** the Boston Massacre.
- **D.** the Battle of Saratoga.

15. The end of the Revolutionary War was marked by
- **A.** the Battle of Saratoga.
- **B.** the ringing of the Liberty Bell.
- **C.** the surrender of General Cornwallis.
- **D.** the signing of the Treaty of Paris.

(continued)

Part Two: Test Your Skills

DIRECTIONS: **Use the map of North America to answer the following questions.**

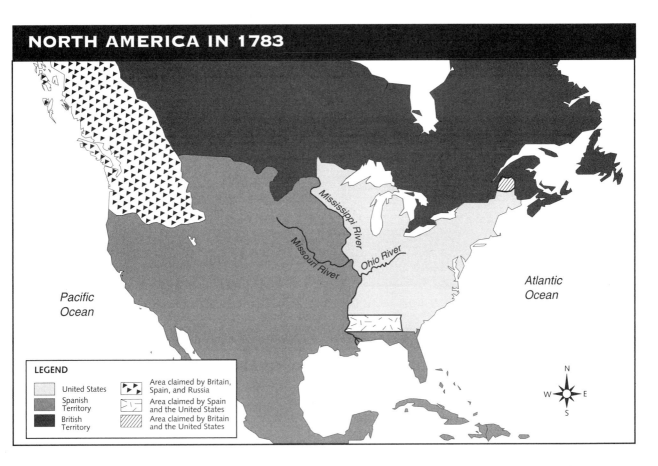

NORTH AMERICA IN 1783

Mississippi River

Missouri River

Ohio River

Pacific Ocean

Atlantic Ocean

LEGEND

United States

Spanish Territory

British Territory

Area claimed by Britain, Spain, and Russia

Area claimed by Spain and the United States

Area claimed by Britain and the United States

N W E S

16. What two countries controlled the most land in North America?

_____

17. What countries claimed land that was also claimed by Russia?

_____

18. What countries claimed land that was also claimed by the United States?

_____

19. What two countries controlled land around the Great Lakes?

_____

20. What countries claimed land on the west coast of North America?

_____

(continued)

Part Three: Apply What You Have Learned

DIRECTIONS: *Complete each of the following activities.*

21. *Who Does Not Belong?*
Listed below are three groups of people. Circle the name of the person in each group who does not belong. Explain why that person does not belong.

WHO DOES NOT BELONG?	EXPLANATION
Paul Revere Crispus Attucks Thomas Gage	
Thomas Jefferson George III Thomas Paine	
Benedict Arnold George Washington Charles Cornwallis	

(continued)

22. Essay

The British army clearly had many advantages over the Continental
army. Write one paragraph analyzing why the Continental army was able
to defeat the powerful British army.

Individual
Performance Task
A Letter Home

Your task is to choose a person who might have taken some part in the Revolutionary War and to write a letter from the point of view of that person.

First, choose one of the following persons:
- a soldier at Valley Forge writing home to his family
- the wife of a shoemaker, spending the winter at Valley Forge with her husband, writing home to their family
- a woman who is running the family farm writing to her husband in the Continental army
- a British soldier writing to his parents after the surrender at Yorktown
- a colonist who watched the Boston Tea Party, writing to a friend in Virginia

Then reread the information in the unit that is about your subject. You may also want to do research in the library to gather additional information. In writing your letter, be sure to include the following:
- events you, as the person writing the letter, have seen or taken part in
- problems you face, both small and large
- people you have met or heard about
- the feelings you have about the things that are happening

Be creative, but keep your letter true to history.

Group
Performance Task
The Declaration of Independence

In the introduction to the Declaration of Independence, Thomas Jefferson explained why the Declaration was being written. The introduction is shown below.

> *When in the Course of human events, it becomes necessary for one people to dissolve the political bands which have connected them with another, and to assume among the powers of the earth, the separate and equal station to which the Laws of Nature and of Nature's God entitle them, a decent respect to the opinions of mankind requires that they should declare the causes which impel them to the separation.*

In this activity, the class will be divided into groups of five students. Each group will rewrite the introduction so that students in a lower grade can understand the reasons for the Declaration. Use dictionaries to find the meanings of the words you do not understand. Discuss in your group the best way to express the ideas in this opening paragraph.

After your group has rewritten the introduction, you may want to present it to students in another class to be sure that they can understand what you have written.

Chapter Test 9

Part One: Test Your Understanding

DIRECTIONS: *Circle the letter of the best answer.*

1. The Articles of Confederation and the Iroquois League were similar in that they both
   A. had a president.
   B. brought together different groups of people.
   C. stated people's desire to declare war on Britain.
   D. were headed by women.

2. A republic is a form of government in which
   A. the people are ruled by a king or queen.
   B. only the wealthy have rights and responsibilities.
   C. all people must pay taxes in order to vote.
   D. the people elect representatives to run the country.

3. Which of these was a part of the national government under the Articles of Confederation?
   A. a national legislature   B. a president
   C. a king   D. a national court system

4. Under the Articles of Confederation, Congress had the authority to
   A. raise a national army.
   B. make laws about taxes.
   C. print money.
   D. elect a single leader to run the government.

5. The purpose of the Northwest Ordinance was to
   A. prevent settlement in the Ohio River valley.
   B. set up a system by which new states could be formed.
   C. ask the states to send delegates to Philadelphia for a convention.
   D. end the troubles caused by Shays's Rebellion.

6. Which of these was a result of the Annapolis Convention of 1786?
   A. Each state started printing its own money.
   B. The Articles of Confederation were written.
   C. Congress created a new national army.
   D. Congress called the Constitutional Convention.

(continued)

7. The delegates to the Constitutional Convention met in
    A. Boston.   **B.** Annapolis.
    C. St. Augustine.   **D.** Philadelphia.

8. In a federal system of government, power and authority
    A. are given to the states.
    B. are shared by the national and state governments.
    C. belong only to the national government.
    D. belong to the people and the states.

9. The Three-fifths Compromise that was reached at the Constitutional Convention involved the
    A. number of British citizens allowed to live in the United States.
    B. number of houses of Congress to be created.
    C. counting of slaves for the purposes of representation and taxation.
    D. amount of power that was to be given to the national government.

10. Under the Constitution, how many senators does each state have?
    A. two   **B.** three
    C. four   **D.** five

11. Which of these is used to determine how many representatives a state will have in the House of Representatives?
    A. the amount the state pays in taxes
    B. the physical size of the state
    C. the number of government branches
    D. the population of the state

12. The branch of government responsible for carrying out the nation's laws is the
    A. executive branch.   **B.** electoral college.
    C. judicial branch.   **D.** legislative branch.

13. The Supreme Court is part of the
    A. legislative branch of the government.
    B. judicial branch of the government.
    C. electoral college.
    D. executive branch of the government.

14. Which of these helps to keep one branch of the government from gaining more power than the other two branches?
    A. the Three-fifths Compromise   **B.** the Preamble to the Constitution
    C. the system of checks and balances **D.** the electoral college

(continued)

Part Two: Test Your Skills

DIRECTIONS: *Delegates at the Constitutional Convention often had trouble agreeing on issues. In order to write a Constitution, the delegates had to make compromises. In the spaces below are three issues related to the Constitution and opposing views on those issues. Describe the compromise that was reached on each issue.*

REPRESENTATION IN CONGRESS	
Virginia Plan: The number of representatives in Congress from each state would be based on state population.	**New Jersey Plan:** Each state would have the same number of representatives in Congress.
15. The Great Compromise	

COUNTING SLAVES	
Northern Plan: Slaves would not be included in state population counts.	**Southern Plan:** Slaves would be included in state population counts.
16. The Three-fifths Compromise	

THE SLAVE TRADE	
Northern Plan: The slave trade would be stopped.	**Southern Plan:** The slave trade would not be stopped.
17. The Compromise Over the Slave Trade	

(continued)

Part Three: Apply What You Have Learned

DIRECTIONS: *Complete each of the following activities.*

18. Constitutional Authority
According to the Constitution, some powers belong to the states, some powers belong to the national government, and some powers are shared by both the states and the national government. In the diagram, list two examples of each kind of power.

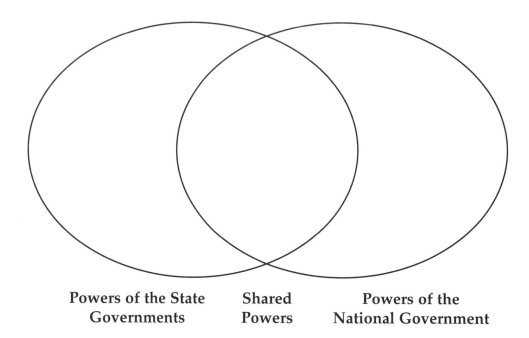

Powers of the State   **Shared**   **Powers of the**
Governments   **Powers**   **National Government**

19. Essay
The delegates to the Constitutional Convention had to make compromises before they could finish writing the Constitution. One of the first compromises they made was the Great Compromise. In a one-paragraph essay, explain what this compromise was about and what its results were.

Chapter Test 10

Part One: Test Your Understanding

DIRECTIONS: *Circle the letter of the best answer.*

1. *The Federalist* was a collection of letters that
  A. created rules for the new government.
  B. set up the method for electing the President.
  C. defended the Constitution.
  D. claimed there was no need for a bill of rights.

2. The First Amendment in the Bill of Rights
  A. protects religious freedom.
  B. creates the electoral college.
  C. gives people the right to have guns.
  D. lets each state have two senators.

3. The right to a fair, public trial with a lawyer is
  A. a check-and-balance power.
  B. due process of law.
  C. part of the federal system.
  D. a responsibility of citizenship.

4. According to the Ninth Amendment, all people have
  A. the right to serve on a jury.
  B. the right to refuse to pay taxes.
  C. basic human rights.
  D. the right to keep and bear arms.

5. President George Washington chose Thomas Jefferson to
  A. build a national army.
  B. advise him on matters of law.
  C. set up a new banking system.
  D. establish ties with leading world powers.

6. The attorney general is the
  A. President's legal adviser.
  B. leader of the army.
  C. leader of the House of Representatives.
  D. most important justice on the Supreme Court.

(continued)

7. Which of these best describes the ideas of Alexander Hamilton?
    A. He wanted most people to live on farms.
    B. He wanted to strengthen the authority of the states.
    C. He wanted close ties with France.
    D. He wanted a strong national government.

8. Members of the Democratic-Republican party supported
    A. John Adams.
    B. Alexander Hamilton.
    C. Thomas Jefferson.
    D. George Washington.

DIRECTIONS: *Match the descriptions on the left with the words or names on the right. Write the correct letter in the space provided.*

9. _____ people who wanted to ratify the Constitution

10. _____ people who agreed to ratify the Constitution only if it included a bill of rights

    A. Fourth Amendment

11. _____ protects the right of free speech

    B. John Adams

    C. Anti-Federalists

12. _____ protects people's homes from unreasonable government searches

    D. Cabinet

    E. Thomas Jefferson

13. _____ advisers to the President

    F. Federalists

14. _____ person whose ideas about government differed greatly from those of Alexander Hamilton

    G. First Amendment

15. _____ first President to live in the White House

(continued)

Part Two: Test Your Skills

DIRECTIONS: *A book cover can be a document that gives information about a publication. Study the cover of* The Federalist *below and answer the questions that follow.*

THE

FEDERALIST:

A COLLECTION

OF

E S S A Y S,

WRITTEN IN FAVOUR OF THE

NEW CONSTITUTION,

AS AGREED UPON BY THE FEDERAL CONVENTION,
SEPTEMBER 17, 1787.

IN TWO VOLUMES.

VOL. I.

N·E W-Y O R K:

PRINTED AND SOLD BY J. AND A. M'LEAN,
No. 41, HANOVER-SQUARE.
M,DCC,LXXXVIII.

16. *The Federalist* is a collection of _____.

17. In what city was *The Federalist* published? _____

18. How many volumes of *The Federalist* were published? _____

19. Does this document make you think many people were in favor of the Constitution?

Explain your answer. _____

_____

_____

20. What do you think the reason was for publishing this collection of essays?

_____

_____

(continued)

Part Three: Apply What You Have Learned

DIRECTIONS: *Complete each of the following activities.*

21. **Leaders of Government**
    Each of the individuals shown on the left did important work in the first government under the Constitution. Draw a line from each person's name to the position he held in the government.

John Jay	Vice President
Alexander Hamilton	Attorney General
Henry Knox	Chief Justice of the Supreme Court
Edmund Randolph	Secretary of War
John Adams	Secretary of the Treasury

22. **Responsibilities of Citizenship**
    The Constitution lists the rights guaranteed to all Americans. The Constitution also suggests the responsibilities of citizenship. List five of these responsibilities.

    a. _____

    b. _____

    c. _____

    d. _____

    e. _____

23. **Essay**
    On March 4, 1797, the second President of the United States took the oath of office. Write a paragraph telling who took the oath of office on that day and why that event marked an important day in history.

NAME _____ DATE _____

Unit 5 Test

Part One: Test Your Understanding

DIRECTIONS: *Circle the letter of the best answer.*

1. The Articles of Confederation limited the authority of Congress by
  A. giving more power to the President.
  B. weakening the power of the states.
  C. creating a republic.
  D. requiring 9 of 13 states to agree before a law is passed.

2. Shays's Rebellion showed people
  A. how to get a law passed by Congress.
  B. the weakness of government under the Articles of Confederation.
  C. the value of making compromises.
  D. why a bill of rights was needed.

3. Making the national government strong without taking away the powers of the states was an accomplishment of
  A. the Constitutional Convention.
  B. the Articles of Confederation.
  C. President Washington and his Cabinet.
  D. the Annapolis Convention.

4. In a federal system of government, power and authority
  A. belong to the President alone.
  B. belong to the national government alone.
  C. belong to the states alone.
  D. are shared by the states and the national government.

5. Who has the authority to veto a bill?
  A. the President   B. the Supreme Court
  C. the Senate   D. the Cabinet

6. The writers of the Constitution made sure no one branch of government could become too powerful by
  A. making the President the leader of all three branches.
  B. creating a system of checks and balances.
  C. creating political parties.
  D. appointing the leader of each branch for life.

(continued)

7. People who were Federalists

    A. supported a weak national government.

    B. wanted the Preamble to the Constitution to begin with "We the States. . . ."

    C. wanted a bill of rights added to the Constitution.

    D. wanted to ratify the Constitution.

8. Which of these was written by Alexander Hamilton, James Madison, and John Jay?

    A. the Articles of Confederation

    B. the Constitution of the United States

    C. *The Federalist*

    D. the Declaration of Independence

9. Freedom of religion, speech, and the press are protected by the

    A. First Amendment.   **B.** Second Amendment.

    C. Fifth Amendment.   **D.** Tenth Amendment.

10. Basic human rights are protected by the

    A. Second Amendment.   **B.** Third Amendment.

    C. Ninth Amendment.   **D.** Tenth Amendment.

11. To help him do the work of the executive branch, the first President of the United States created

    A. a Cabinet.   **B.** a federal system of government.

    C. the Supreme Court.   **D.** a two-house Congress.

12. Creating a strong national government was the goal of

    A. Thomas Jefferson.   **B.** Alexander Hamilton.

    C. James Madison.   **D.** Patrick Henry.

13. The first two political parties in the United States were

    A. the Democratic party and the Republican party.

    B. the Loyalist party and the Patriot party.

    C. the Democratic-Republican party and the Federalist party.

    D. the Tory party and the Loyalist party.

14. Which of these best describes the transfer of the presidency of George Washington to the presidency of John Adams?

    A. It was one of the first times that a nation had changed leaders by peaceful election.

    B. It was a victory for the Anti-Federalist party.

    C. It came at the end of George Washington's third term in office.

    D. It was the first election for President under the Constitution.

(continued)

Part Two: Test Your Skills

DIRECTIONS: *Answer the questions by using your pencil or the edge of a ruler to measure distances on the map of the Mohawk Trail below.*

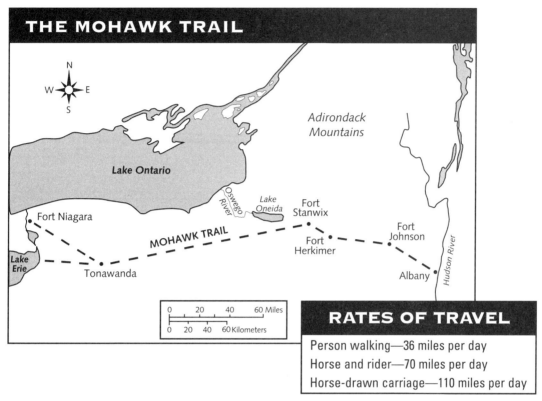

THE MOHAWK TRAIL

RATES OF TRAVEL

Person walking—36 miles per day

Horse and rider—70 miles per day

Horse-drawn carriage—110 miles per day

15. How far is it from Fort Niagara to Tonawanda? How long would it take for a person to travel from Fort Niagara to Tonawanda in a horse-drawn carriage?

_____

16. How long would it take for a person to go by horse from Fort Herkimer to Albany?

_____

17. How long would it take a person to walk from Tonawanda to Fort Stanwix? How long would it take by horse and rider? by horse-drawn carriage?

_____

(continued)

Part Three: Apply What You Have Learned

DIRECTIONS: *Complete each of the following activities.*

18. *The Three Branches of Government*
Fill in the missing information in the chart below.

LEGISLATIVE BRANCH	EXECUTIVE BRANCH	JUDICIAL BRANCH
Purpose:	Purpose:	Purpose:
Two houses:	Leader:	Leading body:
Number in each body today:	How selected:	How selected:

(continued)

19. *Government Under the Constitution*

Fill in the names of the first United States government below.

President	Vice President	Chief Justice
_____	_____	_____

Secretary of State	Secretary of War	Secretary of the Treasury	Attorney General
_____	_____	_____	_____

20. *Essay*

A bill must go through many steps before it becomes a law. Write a paragraph explaining how a bill becomes a law.

Individual Performance Task
Preamble to the United States Constitution

The words of the Preamble to the United States Constitution set forth the goals of the new government. Read the Preamble. Look up in a dictionary any words in the Preamble you do not understand. Discuss with your teacher and classmates the meaning of the Preamble.

> *We the people of the United States, in order to form a more perfect Union, establish justice, insure domestic tranquillity, provide for the common defense, promote the general welfare, and secure the blessings of liberty to ourselves and our posterity, do ordain and establish this Constitution for the United States of America . . .*

Today the national government carries out activities that are designed to fulfill the goals expressed in the Preamble. The basic goals of the government are:
- to form a more perfect union
- to establish justice
- to ensure domestic tranquillity
- to provide for the common defense
- to promote the general welfare
- to secure the blessings of liberty

Write the Preamble in the center of a sheet of art paper or posterboard. Make a collage showing four ways that the government carries out the goals of the Preamble. Use pictures from newspapers and magazines to show these activities, or draw your own pictures. Label each picture to show what goal mentioned in the Preamble is represented.

Group Performance Task
Create a One-Act Play

Use one of the following four topics as the basis for writing a one-act play. There should be between four and six actors in the play, and the play should take 10 to 15 minutes to perform. Gather information about your topic from your textbook, the school library, or both. Try to be both creative and historically accurate in your script.

Topic 1: Government Under the Articles of Confederation

Subject: Describe government under the Articles of Confederation, including its weaknesses and its strengths.

Characters: Narrator, John Dickinson, members of Congress, Daniel Shays, and Alexander Hamilton

Topic 2: The Great Compromise

Subject: Describe the ideas of the large states and of the small states at the Constitutional Convention. What did they want? What plans did they discuss? What was the Great Compromise? What did the large states get? What did the small states get?

Characters: George Washington as the narrator (president of the convention), delegates from the large states, and delegates from the small states

Topic 3: Ratifying the Constitution

Subject: Describe the debate over the ratification of the Constitution. Use the debate and the compromise over a bill of rights as the central point of your play.

Characters: Narrator, Federalists, and Anti-Federalists

Topic 4: The Bill of Rights

Subject: Describe at least five rights of American citizens that are protected by the Bill of Rights.

Characters: Narrator and individual citizens using their rights

Chapter Test 11

Part One: Test Your Understanding

DIRECTIONS: *Circle the letter of the best answer.*

1. To make his way over the mountains into Kentucky, Daniel Boone first tried to find the
    A. Mississippi River.
    B. Louisiana Purchase.
    C. Warrior's Path.
    D. Northwest Passage.

2. When Daniel Boone first went to Kentucky, he found many
    A. wild horses.
    B. trading settlements.
    C. canals.
    D. buffalo.

3. What did Daniel Boone do to help settle the West?
    A. He helped make the Wilderness Road.
    B. He explored the Mississippi River.
    C. He traded goods with people in New Orleans.
    D. He signed a peace treaty with the Cherokees and the Shawnees.

4. One of the first things that pioneer families had to do when they moved to the western frontier was to
    A. build adobe houses.
    B. build missions.
    C. clear thick forests.
    D. set up a government.

5. To stop the United States frontier from moving farther west, Spain
    A. declared war on Tennessee.
    B. closed the port of New Orleans to western farmers.
    C. ordered the Indian tribes to stop trading with Americans.
    D. sent Spanish settlers into Kentucky.

6. How did the Louisiana Purchase change the United States?
    A. It cut the size of the United States in half.
    B. It outlawed slavery in all states east of Louisiana.
    C. It doubled the size of the country.
    D. It increased the number of states in the country to 14.

7. Which of the following people served as a guide for the Lewis and Clark expedition?
    A. Sacagawea
    B. Tecumseh
    C. the Prophet
    D. Cameahwait

(continued)

8. The Lewis and Clark expedition helped later pioneers by
    A. building the National Highway.
    B. mapping passes through the Rockies.
    C. finding a route to the Atlantic Ocean.
    D. clearing the Cumberland Gap.

9. Who wanted to form a strong confederation of Indians in Kentucky and Tennessee?
    A. Andrew Jackson   **B.** William Henry Harrison
    C. Tecumseh   **D.** Sequoyah

10. One result of the Battle of Tippecanoe was that
    A. the Americans and the Indians signed a peace treaty.
    B. the Indians agreed to leave the Northwest Territory.
    C. the Americans agreed to pay the Indians for the cost of the war.
    D. the Americans destroyed Prophetstown.

11. Which of the following groups of Americans did not want the United States to go to war with Britain in 1812?
    A. western farmers   **B.** southern planters
    C. War Hawks   **D.** northern merchants

12. Which of the following was a turning point in the War of 1812?
    A. the battle on Lake Erie
    B. the impressment of American sailors
    C. the formation of the War Hawks
    D. the Battle of New Orleans

13. After the War of 1812, during the Era of Good Feelings, the United States government
    A. was stronger in its dealings with foreign nations.
    B. sent people to explore land gained from France.
    C. was too weak to stop European countries from expanding their American empires.
    D. lost land to Spain and Britain.

14. Who wrote a poem about American bravery as the British bombed Fort McHenry in Baltimore Harbor?
    A. James Monroe   **B.** Francis Scott Key
    C. Meriwether Lewis   **D.** Zebulon Pike

(continued)

Part Two: Test Your Skills

DIRECTIONS: *In this chapter you read about the Louisiana Purchase. President Thomas Jefferson spent $15 million to gain more than 800,000 square miles of land for the United States. You also learned about the Lewis and Clark expedition through the unexplored lands. Think about the history of the United States up to that time. Then make three predictions about what you think will happen to the lands that were part of the Louisiana Purchase.*

THE LOUISIANA PURCHASE

Louisiana
Purchase

PREDICTIONS ABOUT THE LANDS OF THE LOUISIANA PURCHASE	
15. Prediction 1	
16. Prediction 2	
17. Prediction 3	

(continued)

Part Three: Apply What You Have Learned

DIRECTIONS: *Complete each of the following activities.*

18. *National Heroes*

Many people helped develop the United States in the early 1800s. Four of them are listed below. Because of their actions, these people are known as national heroes. In the space provided, briefly explain what each person did to become a national hero.

HERO	WHAT THE PERSON DID
Daniel Boone	
Andrew Jackson	
Francis Scott Key	
Zebulon Pike	

19. *Essay*

One result of the War of 1812 was the growth of nationalism in the United States. Write one paragraph explaining what nationalism is and how it is shown by Americans today.

Chapter Test 12

Part One: Test Your Understanding

DIRECTIONS: *Use a name from the box below to complete each of the sentences that follow.*

> Frederick Douglass   Robert Fulton
>
> Francis Cabot Lowell   Horace Mann
>
> Samuel Slater   Harriet Beecher Stowe

1. A British factory worker named _____ brought the plans for a spinning machine to the United States.

2. _____ built a textile mill in which spinning, dyeing, and weaving all took place in the same factory.

3. _____ built a steamboat that he called the *Clermont.*

4. _____ believed schools should be supported by taxes and should be free and open to all children.

5. _____ wrote *Uncle Tom's Cabin*, which turned many people against slavery.

6. A runaway slave named _____ told many people about his escape from slavery.

DIRECTIONS: *Circle the letter of the best answer.*

7. One thing that helped Andrew Jackson become President in 1828 was the fact that
   A. only people who could read and write were allowed to vote.
   B. married women could vote if they promised to vote the same way as their husbands.
   C. white men no longer had to own property to vote.
   D. free Africans were allowed to vote for the first time.

(continued)

8. Who was responsible for forcing the Cherokees off their land and onto the Trail of Tears?
    A. John Calhoun   **B.** James Monroe
    C. John Marshall   **D.** Andrew Jackson

9. Which of the following statements best describes the idea of Manifest Destiny?
    A. All American citizens should have the right to vote.
    B. All American women should have the right to own property.
    C. The United States should stretch from the Atlantic Ocean to the Pacific Ocean.
    D. All Native Americans should live in the land west of the Mississippi River.

10. In order to practice their religion where no one would bother them, the Mormons settled in what is now
    A. Texas.   **B.** Utah.
    C. Oregon.   **D.** Kansas.

11. The United States purchased California and much more land in the West after it won a war with
    A. Spain.   **B.** France.
    C. Britain.   **D.** Mexico.

12. Forty-niners were people who
    A. wanted to end slavery.
    B. traveled on the Oregon Trail.
    C. went to California to search for gold.
    D. supported the idea of states' rights.

13. Abolitionists worked to
    A. put an end to slavery.
    B. persuade people to use tax money to support schools.
    C. start a war with Mexico.
    D. give women the vote.

14. Which of these people was a former slave who traveled across the United States speaking out against slavery?
    A. Sojourner Truth   **B.** William Lloyd Garrison
    C. Harriet Beecher Stowe   **D.** Horace Mann

(continued)

Part Two: Test Your Skills

DIRECTIONS: *Use the information in the double-bar graph to answer the questions.*

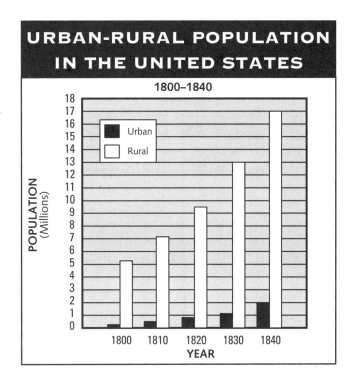

URBAN-RURAL POPULATION IN THE UNITED STATES

1800–1840

15. Between 1800 and 1840, did more people live in urban areas, such as New York City, or in rural areas? _____

16. About how many people lived in rural areas in 1810? _____

17. In which year on the graph did the population in urban areas first pass one million?

_____

18. To the closest million, what was the **total** (urban and rural) population of the United States in 1840? _____

19. The population in both areas grew a lot in the 40 years shown on the graph, but which population grew at the faster rate? _____

(continued)

Part Three: Apply What You Have Learned

DIRECTIONS: *Complete each of the following activities.*

20. *The Industrial Revolution*
The Industrial Revolution brought many changes to the United States.
In the boxes below, list two changes in transportation and two changes
in manufacturing brought about by the Industrial Revolution.

CHANGES IN TRANSPORTATION	CHANGES IN MANUFACTURING

21. *Abolitionists Spread Their Message*
Abolitionists used speakers, newspapers, and books to tell Americans
about slavery. In the chart below, give one example of each method.

METHODS	EXAMPLES
Speakers	
Newspapers	
Books	

22. *Essay*
President Andrew Jackson and Vice President John C. Calhoun
disagreed on the issues of sectionalism and states' rights. Write one
paragraph explaining how the two leaders differed in their views.

Unit 6 Test

Part One: Test Your Understanding

DIRECTIONS: *Circle the letter of the best answer.*

1. Who led American settlers across the Appalachian Mountains into Kentucky?
   A. Meriwether Lewis   **B.** Zebulon Pike
   C. William Clark   **D.** Daniel Boone

2. Which of the following doubled the size of the United States?
   A. the Monroe Doctrine   **B.** the Louisiana Purchase
   C. the War of 1812   **D.** the Erie Canal

3. Which of the following people was responsible for American traders' carrying out an economic invasion of New Mexico?
   A. Zebulon Pike   **B.** Stephen F. Austin
   C. Brigham Young   **D.** Sam Houston

4. As a result of the War of 1812,
   A. France established new colonies in North America.
   B. a wave of nationalism swept the United States.
   C. Spain was added to the United States.
   D. the Americans defeated the British at the Battle of Washington, D.C.

5. The term *mass production* refers to
   A. hiring many people to work in factories.
   B. transporting goods, products, and people by water.
   C. making parts by hand.
   D. producing large amounts of goods at one time.

6. When the Erie Canal was finished, traders could transport goods by water from New York City to
   A. the Great Lakes.   **B.** the Hudson River.
   C. the Mississippi River.   **D.** the Ohio River valley.

7. Horace Mann was a leader in the movement for
   A. women's rights.   **B.** manifest destiny.
   C. public schools.   **D.** mass production.

(continued)

NAME _____ DATE _____

DIRECTIONS: *Match the description on the left with the correct name on the right. Write the correct letter in the space provided.*

8. _____ the name for the pass through the Appalachian Mountains into Kentucky

9. _____ the person who brought the plans for a spinning machine to the United States

A. Robert Fulton

10. _____ the Shoshone woman who acted as a translator for the Lewis and Clark expedition

B. Andrew Jackson

C. Cumberland Gap

11. _____ the abolitionist speaker who was a runaway slave

D. Stephen F. Austin

12. _____ the person who invented the first steam-powered boat

E. Samuel Slater

F. Frederick Douglass

13. _____ the person who established a colony of Americans in Texas

G. Sacagawea

14. _____ the American President who ignored the Supreme Court's ruling about the protection of the Cherokees

(continued)

Part Two: Test Your Skills

DIRECTIONS: Use the information in the maps below to answer the questions.

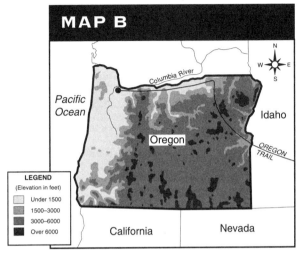

15. What physical feature did the people using the Oregon Trail want to avoid?

_____

16. Across what type of land did the people using the Oregon Trail hope to travel?

_____

17. What is the highest elevation crossed by the Oregon Trail in Oregon? What is the

lowest elevation? _____

_____

18. Why did the Oregon Trail not go straight across Oregon to the Pacific Ocean?

_____

_____

(continued)

Part Three: Apply What You Have Learned

DIRECTIONS: *Complete each of the following activities.*

19. *Label the Map*

Use the map below to locate each of the items that follow. Show the location of each item by writing its letter on the map.

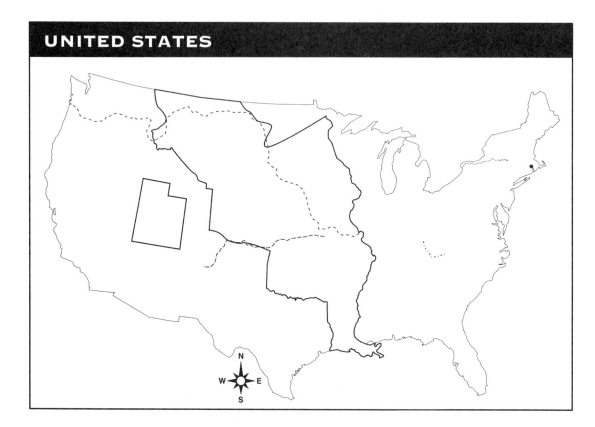

a. the area purchased from France by Thomas Jefferson in 1803

b. the place where Brigham Young and the Mormons settled

c. the path taken by Lewis and Clark

d. the location of Samuel Slater's textile mill

e. the Wilderness Road

f. the Erie Canal

g. the Santa Fe Trail

(continued)

21. *Essay*

In the early 1800s, there were several conflicts between the United States and Britain that led to the War of 1812. Write a paragraph describing one of those conflicts.

Individual Performance Task
Life on the Road

During the nineteenth century many people moved west from where they were living in the United States to start all over in a new place with new opportunities. In this activity you will create a diary for a person who moved west with his or her family.

Step 1 Select one of the following events as the basis for your diary:
- traveling with Daniel Boone to Kentucky
- traveling with Marcus and Narcissa Whitman to the Oregon Country
- traveling with Brigham Young to Utah

Step 2 Use a blank outline map of the United States to draw the route taken by the group you have chosen.

Step 3 Use your textbook and library resources to research the actions of your group.

Step 4 Write at least five diary entries for different events on different days and locations of the journey. Mention who is with you, the geography of the area you are passing through (landforms, vegetation, climate, and wildlife), and some of the events and activities of your daily life. You should be as creative as you can but remain historically accurate.

Step 5 Make a cover for your diary, and share the diary with your classmates.

Group Performance Task
Traveling West

A mobile is a piece of sculpture that hangs balanced in midair. Air currents cause the mobile to move. In this task your group will make a mobile that shows the paths taken by certain groups of settlers as they moved west.

Step 1 You will work in a group of at least five students.

Step 2 Your group should select one of the following:
- Daniel Boone and settlers going through the Cumberland Gap into Kentucky
- Brigham Young and the Mormons going to Utah
- the forty-niners heading for the California gold mines
- travelers along the Erie Canal
- Lewis and Clark exploring the lands of the Louisiana Purchase
- Marcus and Narcissa Whitman going to the Oregon Country
- travelers along the National Road
- Stephen F. Austin going to Texas to set up a colony

Step 3 Make a map showing the route of the group of settlers chosen. Draw a picture that shows some event or location connected with that group. Each member of your group should show a different scene.

Step 4 Paste your map and picture on both sides of a single sheet of construction paper.

Step 5 Use a coat hanger and string to create a mobile. Properly balance each person's artwork so that the mobile will move when it is hit by an air current. Hang the mobiles where others in the school can see them.

Chapter Test 13

Part One: Test Your Understanding

DIRECTIONS: *Circle the letter of the best answer.*

1. The biggest farms in the South were located
  - **A.** near salt marshes.
  - **B.** along the Coastal Plain.
  - **C.** far from the Mississippi River.
  - **D.** near many factories.

2. Most of the people who lived in the South lived
  - **A.** on small farms.
  - **B.** in the cities.
  - **C.** on plantations.
  - **D.** along the sea coast.

3. In the early 1800s, life in the North changed more than life in the South because
  - **A.** slavery became more important.
  - **B.** the number of factories and cities increased.
  - **C.** plantations became more popular.
  - **D.** farmers raised more crops.

4. The invention of the cotton gin by Eli Whitney
  - **A.** caused most of the textile mills in the North to close down.
  - **B.** increased the need for slaves.
  - **C.** decreased the need for cotton.
  - **D.** made people move away from plantations.

5. The most serious disagreement between the North and the South concerned
  - **A.** how much money farmers in the South should be paid for their crops.
  - **B.** whether slavery should be allowed to spread to the frontier.
  - **C.** how best to deal with the Indian peoples living in the North.
  - **D.** whether to pay Eli Whitney for the invention of the cotton gin.

6. Slaves helped each other deal with their daily hardships by
  - **A.** electing leaders to represent them.
  - **B.** demanding that plantation owners pay them more money.
  - **C.** keeping their traditions alive.
  - **D.** writing letters of protest to the President.

(continued)

7. Who helped runaway slaves escape on the Underground Railroad?
  A. Dred Scott
  C. Jefferson Davis
  B. Nat Turner
  D. Harriet Tubman

8. Who persuaded Congress to agree to the Missouri Compromise?
  A. Henry Clay
  C. Stephen Douglas
  B. Abraham Lincoln
  D. Frederick Douglass

9. The Compromise of 1850
  A. encouraged western states to allow slavery.
  B. kept the number of free and slave states equal.
  C. required people to return runaway slaves to the South.
  D. limited the production of cotton.

10. The Kansas-Nebraska Act
  A. outlawed slavery in both Kansas and Nebraska.
  B. led to fighting in Kansas between people for and against slavery.
  C. gave the vote to slaves living in these two places.
  D. offered public education to slaves living in Kansas and Nebraska.

11. In the case of Dred Scott, the Supreme Court ruled that
  A. Scott was property and should not be given his freedom.
  B. slavery should be outlawed in the United States.
  C. slaves should have the same rights as other American citizens.
  D. Congress had the right to outlaw slavery in the Wisconsin Territory.

12. Abraham Lincoln joined the Republican party in order to
  A. make sure each state could decide the slavery question for itself.
  B. run for the U.S. House of Representatives.
  C. fight against the spread of slavery.
  D. work with Stephen Douglas.

13. Shortly after Lincoln was elected President in 1860, a group of Southern states
  A. withdrew from the Union and formed their own country.
  B. agreed to abolish slavery in the next five years.
  C. made plans to stop the spread of slavery to the new states.
  D. passed laws to protect the rights of slaves.

14. The president of the Confederacy was
  A. Jefferson Davis.
  C. Roger B. Taney.
  B. James Forten.
  D. Eli Whitney.

(continued)

Part Two: Test Your Skills

DIRECTIONS: *Use the graph below to answer the questions that follow.*

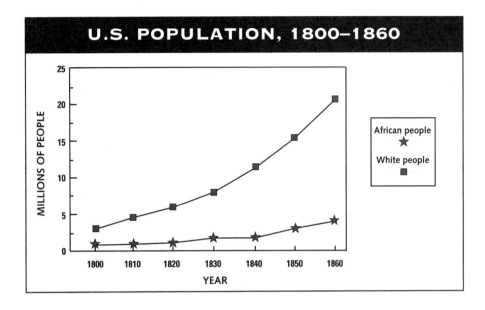

U.S. POPULATION, 1800–1860

15. Approximately how many African people were living in the United States in 1860?

_____

16. In which decade did the population of white people increase the most?

_____

17. Based on this graph, what was the **total** population of white people and African people in the United States in 1860?

_____

18. What conclusions can you draw from this graph?

_____

_____

_____

_____

(continued)

Part Three: Apply What You Have Learned

DIRECTIONS: *Complete each of the following activities.*

19. *The Slave Codes*

Most states in the South in 1860 had slave codes, laws that shaped the day-to-day lives of enslaved people. List three ways that the lives of slaves were shaped by these slave codes.

_____

_____

_____

20. *What Do They Have in Common?*

Listed below are famous people who lived during the 1800s. Form four pairs of people and explain why you grouped them.

General Beauregard	John Brown	Henry Clay
Jefferson Davis	Stephen Douglas	Abraham Lincoln
Harriet Tubman	Nat Turner	Eli Whitney

Pairs of People   **Reason for Placing Them Together**

_____   _____

_____   _____

_____   _____

_____   _____

21. *Essay*

Stephen Douglas and Abraham Lincoln had very different ideas about how the question of slavery should be settled. Write a paragraph explaining how the two men differed in their viewpoints concerning slavery.

Chapter Test 14

Part One: Test Your Understanding

DIRECTIONS: *Circle the letter of the best answer.*

1. What new state was formed out of a slave state by people who were against slavery and wanted to remain in the Union?

   A. Alabama
   C. Nebraska
   B. Kansas
   D. West Virginia

2. An early Northern plan for fighting the war was based on

   A. invading the border states.
   B. having Indian allies capture the Confederate capital.
   C. cutting off Southern trade by setting up a blockade.
   D. invading Georgia and Alabama by sea.

3. The Confederate states

   A. hoped to keep the war only in the South.
   B. hoped that Britain and France would help them fight the war.
   C. had more people, factories, and railroads than the Northern states.
   D. welcomed all women who wanted to become soldiers.

4. Which of the following happened when President Abraham Lincoln signed the Emancipation Proclamation?

   A. Great Britain and France were allowed to buy Southern cotton.
   B. Most of the border states switched sides and joined the Confederacy.
   C. The Union fought against both the Confederacy and slavery.
   D. All of the slaves in the United States were freed.

5. General Grant's victory in the siege of Vicksburg was important because

   A. it was the first battle won by the Union army.
   B. it strengthened the Confederate army.
   C. it gave the Union control of the Mississippi River.
   D. it caused the South to surrender and end the Civil War.

6. In the Gettysburg Address, President Abraham Lincoln

   A. issued the Emancipation Proclamation and freed the slaves.
   B. honored the soldiers who had died fighting for liberty and equality.
   C. named General Ulysses S. Grant to lead the Union army.
   D. created the Freedmen's Bureau to help Africans in the South.

(continued)

7. "The soldiers did not have enough food. Many of them were nearly starving. Their clothes were dirty and torn." This statement best describes
    A. Confederate troops just before General Lee surrendered.
    B. Union troops at the end of the siege of Vicksburg.
    C. Confederate troops after they captured Savannah, Georgia.
    D. Union troops at the Battle of Gettysburg.

8. Which of these events happened **last**?
    A. President Lincoln was assassinated.
    B. General Lee surrendered to General Grant at Appomattox.
    C. The Civil War ended.
    D. General Sherman destroyed the city of Atlanta.

9. Slavery in the United States was ended forever by the passage of the
    A. First Amendment.
    B. Fourteenth Amendment.
    C. Freedmen's Bureau.
    D. Thirteenth Amendment.

10. The most important work of the Freedmen's Bureau was
    A. helping former slaves find their family members.
    B. helping former slaves find jobs in Northern factories.
    C. educating the newly freed slaves.
    D. making loans to the newly freed slaves so that they could buy plantations.

11. The black codes were laws that
    A. limited the freedom of African Americans.
    B. gave African Americans their own land to farm.
    C. made African Americans citizens of the United States.
    D. allowed African Americans to travel freely throughout the United States.

DIRECTIONS: Match the person on the left with the description on the right. Write the correct letter in the space provided.

12. _____ Clara Barton   **A.** led Union soldiers through Georgia on the March to the Sea

13. _____ William T. Sherman   **B.** became President after the assassination of Abraham Lincoln

14. _____ Andrew Johnson   **C.** helped sick and wounded Union soldiers during the Civil War

(continued)

Part Two: Test Your Skills

DIRECTIONS: *You learned about the problems and the difficult decisions Abraham Lincoln and Jefferson Davis had to make as supplies ran out at Fort Sumter. The first chart shows how Lincoln might have made his decision. Imagine you are Jefferson Davis. Use what you have learned about making decisions and about Fort Sumter to complete the second chart.*

PROBLEM: FORT SUMTER MIGHT SURRENDER TO THE SOUTH.	
Possible Solutions:	**Consequence of Each Solution:**
Send supplies to the fort.	Southerners might attack the fort.
Send troops to the fort.	Southerners would surely attack the fort.
Do nothing at all.	After a while, the fort would surrender to the South.
Decision: Send supplies and wait to see what happens.	

PROBLEM: LINCOLN HAS ANNOUNCED THAT HE WILL SEND SUPPLY SHIPS TO FORT SUMTER.	
Possible Solutions:	**Consequence of Each Solution:**
15. Attack the fort **after** the supply ships arrive.	_____ _____
16. Attack the fort **before** the supply ships arrive.	_____ _____ _____
17. Do nothing at all.	_____ _____ _____
18. **Decision:**	

(continued)

Part Three: Apply What You Have Learned

DIRECTIONS: *Complete each of the following activities.*

19. *Famous People*

Listed below are the names of famous people who played a role in the Civil War and Reconstruction. Form two groups of names that go together. A group must have at least two names in it. You may use a name in more than one group. After you form a group, write a brief explanation of why you formed that group. An example has been done for you.

Clara Barton	Ulysses S. Grant	Andrew Johnson
Robert E. Lee	Abraham Lincoln	William H. Seward
William T. Sherman	Sally Tomkins	Harriet Tubman

Example: Lee, Grant — Civil War generals

_____

_____

_____

20. *Essay*

Imagine that you are Robert E. Lee. Last night, April 18, 1861, President Lincoln asked you to take command of the Union army. Shortly after that, you learned that your home state of Virginia had seceded from the Union. You thought long and hard about whether you should accept Lincoln's offer. Write an entry for April 19, 1861, in your journal about your decision.

Unit 7 Test

Part One: Test Your Understanding

DIRECTIONS: *Circle the letter of the best answer.*

1. Why was slavery important in the Southern states?
- **A.** Slaves were needed to produce cotton and other crops.
- **B.** Southern factories depended on slave labor.
- **C.** Slaves were the only people who could read and write.
- **D.** Slaves were needed to build the railroads.

2. Both Nat Turner and John Brown
- **A.** helped Henry Clay with the Missouri Compromise.
- **B.** led slave rebellions.
- **C.** helped runaway slaves get to Northern cities.
- **D.** were free Africans living in New Orleans.

3. People living in the slave communities helped each other cope with hardships by
- **A.** making sure they were paid for their work.
- **B.** electing leaders to represent them.
- **C.** writing rules for all slaves to follow.
- **D.** keeping their traditions alive.

4. The Underground Railroad was important because it
- **A.** brought Northern products to the Southern states.
- **B.** helped slaves escape from the South.
- **C.** carried Southern cotton to the Northern textile mills.
- **D.** was a low-cost way for all Southerners to travel.

5. Before the Civil War, most free Africans
- **A.** lived on Southern plantations.
- **B.** could vote and run for office.
- **C.** faced difficulties in making a living.
- **D.** moved to the western frontier states.

6. The Missouri Compromise
- **A.** forced seven states to leave the Union.
- **B.** made California a state.
- **C.** stopped the activities on the Underground Railroad.
- **D.** kept the number of free states and slave states equal.

(continued)

7. The Missouri Compromise and the Compromise of 1850
   A. tried to settle the question of slavery in the western states.
   B. limited the production of cotton.
   C. were both written by Stephen Douglas.
   D. allowed runaway slaves to live in the free states.

8. The Kansas-Nebraska Act led to
   A. the decision to allow two more free states to join the Union.
   B. the decision to allow Dred Scott to become a United States citizen.
   C. passage of the Compromise of 1850.
   D. violence between people who supported slavery and those who opposed it.

9. Which of the following statements best describes Abraham Lincoln's view on slavery before he became President?
   A. He wanted to end slavery in the South.
   B. He believed the framers of the Constitution wanted slavery to continue.
   C. He was against the spread of slavery to new states.
   D. He wanted to send runaway slaves back to Southern states.

10. Why was the battle at Fort Sumter important?
   A. It showed how strong the Union army was.
   B. It demonstrated the importance of sea power.
   C. It was caused by the assassination of President Lincoln.
   D. It marked the start of the Civil War.

11. Those states that remained in the Union after the Civil War started and that still allowed slavery were called
   A. slave states.   **B.** rebel states.
   C. Confederate states.   **D.** border states.

12. The First Battle of Bull Run was important because it demonstrated that the South
   A. had very poor military leaders.
   B. could only win battles fought on its own territory.
   C. was more powerful than the North had expected.
   D. had difficulty getting enough soldiers for its army.

13. Which of the following statements about African American soldiers in the Civil War is correct?
   A. Fewer than 1,000 Africans served in the Union army.
   B. Africans bravely served and died in many battles.
   C. Many Africans served in the Confederate army.
   D. The Emancipation Proclamation prevented Africans from serving in the army.

(continued)

14. The Confederacy was cut into two parts after the Union victory at the Battle of

    A. Gettysburg.   **B.** Manassas Junction.

    C. Vicksburg.   **D.** Savannah.

15. After the Civil War, the Freedmen's Bureau was established to

    A. return plantations to their former owners.

    B. give African Americans the right to vote.

    C. encourage African Americans to move North.

    D. build schools and educate former slaves.

16. Many members of Congress wanted to change President Johnson's plan for Reconstruction because

    A. they wanted to be more fair to the Southern states than Johnson had been.

    B. they agreed with the black codes.

    C. Johnson had been impeached.

    D. former slaves in some Southern states were being treated harshly.

(continued)

Part Two: Test Your Skills

DIRECTIONS: *Use the maps below to answer the questions that follow.*

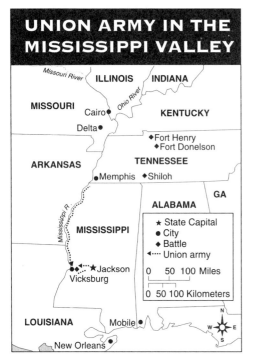

Map 1

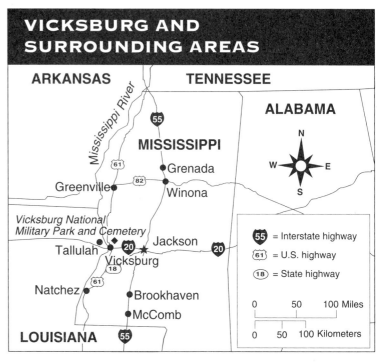

Map 2

17. What is the distance between Memphis and Vicksburg on Map 1?

_____

18. What is the distance between Vicksburg and Jackson on Map 1?

_____ on Map 2? _____

19. Which cities on Map 2 did the Union army probably pass through during the siege of Vicksburg?

_____

20. Which map would you use if you wanted to visit Vicksburg? Explain.

_____

(continued)

Part Three: Apply What You Have Learned

DIRECTIONS: *Complete each of the following activities.*

21. Protesting Slavery

Describe three methods used by enslaved people to protest slavery.

a. _____

_____

b. _____

_____

c. _____

_____

22. Essay

Imagine that you are the son or daughter of a conductor on the Underground Railroad. Write a letter to your closest friend, describing your family's experiences while taking part in the work of the Underground Railroad.

Individual Performance Task
Gettysburg Time Capsule

A *time capsule* is a sealed container that holds articles and/or written documents that are representative of a specific time period and place. A time capsule is buried and preserved by people in one time period for people in a future age.

On November 19, 1863, President Abraham Lincoln went to Gettysburg, Pennsylvania, to dedicate the national cemetery for the soldiers who had died during the Battle of Gettysburg. A special memorial was built to honor the individuals who had fought so bravely in the battle. A time capsule was buried near that memorial. Your task is to imagine that you are in charge of the time capsule. As the person in charge, you must do two things:

- Select six items that will go into the time capsule.
- Explain why you have chosen each item.

These items should be representative of the time period of the Civil War. They should be items that would help someone in today's world better understand the events of the Civil War and the men and women who were alive at that time. Your teacher will tell you what resources you may use to decide what you would put into the time capsule.

Time-Capsule Items   **Reasons for Including Them**

_____   _____

_____   _____

_____   _____

_____   _____

_____   _____

Group Performance Task
You Are There

Radio stations often have news and current-events programs in which a reporter speaks with two or three different people to get their reactions and opinions about a specific individual or event. In this task the class will be divided into groups of four or five students. Each group will create a script of a radio news interview that might have taken place at the end of the Civil War.

One member of each group will act as the radio news reporter, and the other members will act as different people who were living at the end of the Civil War. Together, group members will create a set of written questions for the reporter to ask and a set of written answers to the questions. Then you will present your material to the class as if it were a live radio broadcast. Be sure that your script is representative of the people and the time period immediately following the war.

The people who might be included in your group are:
- a former slave
- a Northern soldier
- an African who served in the Union army
- a Southern soldier
- Clara Barton
- President Andrew Johnson
- General Ulysses S. Grant
- General Robert E. Lee
- Harriet Tubman

The questions that the radio reporter might ask are:
- What are your feelings and emotions at the end of the war?
- What political events during the war were important to you?
- What financial problems do you have today?
- What happened to your family during the war?
- How has the war changed your community?
- What do you think the future will bring for the country?

Chapter Test 15

Part One: Test Your Understanding

DIRECTIONS: *Match the description on the left with the correct word or name on the right. Write the correct letter in the space provided.*

1. _____ economic system in which people are able to start and run their own businesses

2. _____ money needed to run a business

3. _____ business that sells shares of stock to investors

4. _____ person who takes a chance by opening up a business

5. _____ what made many inland cities important centers of industry

6. _____ what workers did to get factory owners to listen to them

7. _____ group of workers who take action to improve their working conditions

8. _____ organization made up of many groups

9. _____ a city neighborhood of Spanish-speaking people

10. _____ what many people born in America feared they would lose to immigrants

11. _____ entry place into the United States for most immigrants from Europe

A. free enterprise

B. Ellis Island

C. railroad

D. corporation

E. skyscrapers

F. barrio

G. trolley car

H. federation

I. capital resources

J. jobs

K. naturalization

L. strike

M. entrepreneur

N. settlement houses

O. labor union

(continued)

12. _____ way for immigrants to become United States citizens

13. _____ community centers in cities that helped immigrants learn skills

14. _____ steel-framed buildings that helped cities grow upward

15. _____ invention that helped make it possible for more people to move to suburbs

(continued)

NAME _____ DATE _____

Part Two: Test Your Skills

DIRECTIONS: *Use the time zone map below to answer the questions that follow.*

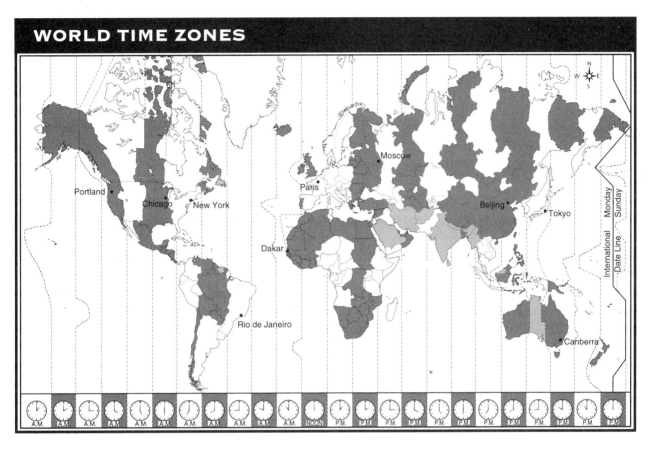

WORLD TIME ZONES

16. When it is 4:00 P.M. in Rio de Janeiro, what time is it in Chicago? _____

17. When it is 7:00 A.M. in New York, what time is it in Moscow? _____

18. When it is 10:00 A.M. in Tokyo, what time is it in Paris? _____

19. When it is 7:00 A.M. in Portland, what time is it in Beijing? _____

(continued)

Part Three: Apply What You Have Learned

DIRECTIONS: *Complete each of the following activities.*

20. *Becoming a Citizen*

Many immigrants felt that becoming United States citizens was very important. To become a citizen, an immigrant had to complete a series of steps. List these steps below.

a. _____

b. _____

c. _____

21. *Essay*

At the end of the nineteenth century and the beginning of the twentieth century, factory workers and new immigrants living in American cities faced many problems. Choose one of these groups and explain in one paragraph the problems they faced living and working in the cities.

CHAPTER 15 TEST

Chapter Test 16

Part One: Test Your Understanding

DIRECTIONS: *Circle the letter of the best answer.*

1. The purpose of the Homestead Act was to
    A. give companies money to build a railroad across the country.
    B. encourage people to settle on the Great Plains.
    C. open the first cattle trail to the railroads.
    D. end the battles between ranchers and farmers.

2. Railroad owners wanted more people to settle on the Great Plains because
    A. settlers would use the railroads for travel.
    B. they needed more people to build railroad tracks.
    C. they needed sharecroppers to farm the land owned by the railroads.
    D. settlers would grow cotton and ship it to the South.

3. Settlers on the Great Plains used sod to build their houses because
    A. sod houses were cleaner than other buildings.
    B. there were few trees that could be used for wood.
    C. houses made from wood were too cold in the winters on the Great Plains.
    D. the railroads paid people to live in sod houses.

4. The person who invented a stronger plow to help people cut through the thick sod was
    A. Joseph Glidden.   **B.** Richard King.
    C. James Oliver.   **D.** George Custer.

5. Which of the following caused some farmers to leave their farms on the Great Plains?
    A. railroads   **B.** bad weather
    C. immigrants   **D.** barbed wire

6. After Joseph McCoy opened his stockyards near some railroad tracks in Abilene, Kansas,
    A. many farmers moved to the Great Plains.
    B. the Indians started moving to the reservations.
    C. ranchers started moving herds of cattle to the "cow towns."
    D. the mining boom in the West ended.

(continued)

7. What were long drives?

    A. transportation by railroad

    B. special areas of farmland on the Great Plains given to homesteaders

    C. the path of the buffalo migration on the Great Plains

    D. trips on which cowhands moved large numbers of cattle to the railroads

8. The range wars were caused by

    A. the use of barbed wire.   **B.** the British.

    C. the steel plow.   **D.** railroad owners.

9. What happened during a mining boom?

    A. Most people lost all of their money.

    B. People moved away from mining areas.

    C. Gold, silver, and copper mines were closed.

    D. There was quick economic growth.

10. Which of the following caused some mining towns to become ghost towns?

    A. The range wars destroyed all the buildings in the towns.

    B. The mines ran out of gold, silver, or copper.

    C. The railroads moved away.

    D. The vaqueros ordered everyone to leave the towns.

11. Law and order was maintained in the mining towns by

    A. the United States Army.   **B.** county sheriffs.

    C. Vigilance Committees.   **D.** the Union army.

12. The most important resource of the Plains Indians was

    A. the buffalo.   **B.** wheat.

    C. the horse.   **D.** corn.

13. Why did General George Custer take his soldiers to the Little Bighorn River in 1876?

    A. to open a new railroad through the Black Hills

    B. to protect cowhands on long drives across the Sioux reservation

    C. to help miners in a boom town

    D. to take back land the government had given to the Sioux

14. Why did U.S. Army soldiers chase the Nez Perces for more than 1,700 miles?

    A. because the Nez Perces were living on land that contained gold

    B. to punish them for defeating Custer and his soldiers

    C. because the Nez Perces were trying to escape to Canada

    D. to stop them from going to war with the Sioux

(continued)

Part Two: Test Your Skills

DIRECTIONS: *Use the climographs to answer the questions that follow.*

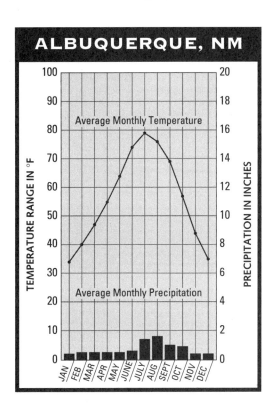

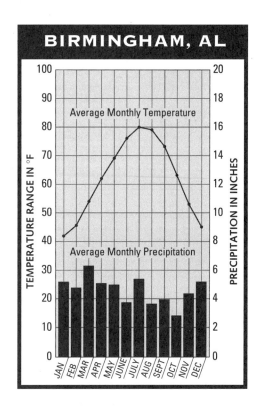

15. What is the wettest month in each city?

_____

16. What is the average temperature in each city in April?

_____

17. What is the coldest month in each city?

_____

18. What is the warmest month in each city?

_____

19. Which city receives more precipitation? _____

(continued)

Part Three: Apply What You Have Learned

DIRECTIONS: *Complete each of the following activities.*

20. *Indian Reservations*

Indian reservations were created by the United States government as places where the Native American peoples could live. Describe how each of the groups below resisted living on reservations.

Sioux

_____

_____

Nez Perces

_____

_____

Apaches

_____

_____

21. *Essay*

The western part of the United States was settled mainly by farmers and miners. Explain in one paragraph how farmers and miners were alike and how they were different.

Unit 8 Test

Part One: Test Your Understanding

DIRECTIONS: *Circle the letter of the best answer.*

1. Which of the following was the first kind of business to set up corporations?
   A. bonanza farms
   B. railroads
   C. steel mills
   D. refining

2. With the growth of industries such as steel and oil, new industrial cities developed
   A. near good harbors.
   B. in the West.
   C. near the oceans.
   D. inland.

3. To try to improve their working conditions, workers in the late 1800s sometimes
   A. fought against the labor unions.
   B. volunteered to be fired so that family members would be hired.
   C. went on strike.
   D. offered to work longer hours for less pay.

4. What were the two basic goals of the American Federation of Labor?
   A. to end strikes and hire more children as workers
   B. to get a five-day workweek and summer vacations
   C. to get higher wages and a shorter workday
   D. to do away with accident insurance and hire fewer children as workers

5. Many Americans wanted to stop the immigration of Asians because
   A. they worried that Asian immigrants would take their jobs.
   B. they did not want the Asian immigrants to create any more barrios in the Southwest.
   C. the law required that Asian immigrants be paid more than other people.
   D. the eastern part of the United States was becoming too crowded.

6. During the early 1900s, many African American families moved to the northern cities because
   A. they wanted to get better land to farm.
   B. they were forced to leave the southern states.
   C. the climate in the North was better.
   D. there were more jobs in the northern cities.

(continued)

7. What was the purpose of a settlement house?
  A. to give cowhands a place to stay after the cattle drives
  B. to help immigrants learn American skills and customs
  C. to teach farmers about irrigation
  D. to improve the education of schoolteachers

8. Many settlers in the West bought land at low prices from the
  A. Indians.   **B.** vaqueros.
  C. railroads.   **D.** miners.

9. Most houses on the Great Plains were made with
  A. adobe.   **B.** bricks.
  C. sod.   **D.** logs.

10. It was important for ranchers to get their cattle to northern cities because
  A. people in the southern cities did not eat beef.
  B. all the cattle buyers in the country lived in the North.
  C. northern cities had more open range in which to raise cattle.
  D. they could earn a higher profit in the northern cities.

11. How did Joseph Glidden help to bring an end to the Cattle Kingdom?
  A. He made the first steel plow.
  B. He founded the first mining town.
  C. He invented barbed wire.
  D. He built the first transcontinental railroad.

12. When did mining towns experience the most rapid population growth?
  A. when windmills were invented
  B. when people moved away from the mines
  C. when the gold, silver, and copper mines closed
  D. when there was quick economic growth

13. The traditional way of life of the Plains Indians came to an end when
  A. the cattle drives began.   **B.** the range wars ended.
  C. settlers killed off the buffalo. **D.** the mining boom started.

14. Geronimo and his people refused to stay on the reservation because
  A. they wanted to return to the Black Hills of South Dakota.
  B. there was not enough food on their reservation.
  C. there was no railroad on their reservation.
  D. they wanted to follow the buffalo on their migration.

(continued)

Part Two: Test Your Skills

DIRECTIONS: *Problem solving is an important skill. Homesteaders on the Great Plains faced many problems as they made a new life in this region. One of the problems they had to solve was that of getting water for their families and their animals. For each possible solution to the problem listed in the table below, give reasons as to why it is a good solution or why it is a bad solution.*

SOLVING A PROBLEM	
Problem: Getting water to the farms on the Great Plains	
Possible Solution	Results of Solution
15. Build pipelines to carry water from rivers to the farms.	
16. Build dams on streams to store water for the farms.	
17. Bring in water by wagons or by railroads to the farms.	
18. Build windmills to pump water from the ground for the farms.	

(continued)

Part Three: Apply What You Have Learned

DIRECTIONS: *Complete each of the following activities.*

19. **Magic Square**
    From the statements below, select the best match for each name listed.
    Put the number of the name with the matching statement letter in the
    magic square. You can check your answers by adding across each row or
    down each column. You should get the same number each way. Record
    that number in the magic number space.

a = _____	b = _____	c = _____
d = _____	e = _____	f = _____
g = _____	h = _____	i = _____

1. Sitting Bull
2. Samuel Gompers
3. George Westinghouse
4. William Jenney
5. Henry Bessemer
6. Chief Joseph
7. Joseph McCoy
8. Jane Addams
9. James Oliver

Magic Number = _____

a. started the American Federation of Labor

b. built the first skyscraper

c. invented a steel plow that helped farmers on the Great Plains

d. built the stockyards at Abilene, Kansas, that started the cattle drives

e. invented the safety brake for trains

f. created a new, improved process for making steel

g. led the Nez Perces on an escape to Canada

h. started Hull House in Chicago to teach new skills to immigrants

i. led the Sioux at the Battle of Little Bighorn

(continued)

20. *Essay*

The government had different policies toward unions, immigrants, and Indians at the end of the nineteenth century. Choose one of these groups. Explain in one paragraph the government's policy toward that group.

Individual Performance Task
Have We Got a Deal for You!

Many businesses use a brochure to advertise to the public. In this task you are going to create a brochure that could have been used by one of the transcontinental railroads to get people to move into the areas along its path.

Step 1 Use library materials and your textbooks to find the paths of the first four transcontinental railroads (Northern Pacific, Union Pacific-Central Pacific, Santa Fe, and Southern Pacific). Select one of these railroads. Then select an area along the railroad that you will advertise in the brochure.

Step 2 Decide who will read the brochure. Will it be people immigrating to the United States? Will it be people who want to move from the East to the West? The information you give will depend on who your readers will be.

Step 3 Determine what information you will put in the brochure. You must include the name and address of the railroad company and a map of the area you are advertising. You should also tell in the brochure what is good about the area you are advertising. You might cover some of these topics and add others of your own.

- climate
- mineral resources
- religious freedom
- water resources
- crops
- political freedom
- lumber resources
- wild animals
- land prices
- soil
- plants

Step 4 Make a rough draft of the brochure. Put information on the front of the brochure that will make people want to open it and read further. Draw the map on the back of the brochure, along with the name and address of the railroad company. (You do not have to use a real address. Make up an address in the area you are advertising.) After you have made the rough draft, show it to a classmate and ask whether all the material is clear.

Step 5 Make a final copy. Present the brochure to the rest of the class.

Group Performance Task
Words of the Old West

A *lexicon* is a collection of words. In this task your small group will create a book called *A Lexicon of the Old West.*

Step 1　With your group, brainstorm words from *A* to *Z* that deal with the West as covered in this unit. The words should be about farmers, ranchers, cowhands, miners, and Indians during the last years of the nineteenth century. For example, an *A* word might be *Abilene* and a *B* word might be *Bonanza Farm*. The letter does not have to be the first letter of the word. For example, an *X* word could be *Sioux*. Try to come up with as many words for each letter as possible.

Step 2　Help your group choose one word for each letter of the alphabet. It should be one for which a picture could be drawn to show its meaning or importance.

Step 3　Divide the letters of the alphabet among the members of the group. Each person should be responsible for about the same number of letters. Each student will create a page for the lexicon for each of his or her words. There should be three parts to each page.

> **Part 1**　At the top of the page will be the words *A is for Abilene, B is for Bonanza Farm*, and so on.
>
> **Part 2**　In the center of the page will be a drawing that shows the meaning of the word. For example, under *A is for Abilene* could be a drawing of a railroad train, a stockyard, and cattle being loaded on the train.
>
> **Part 3**　At the bottom of the page will be a two-sentence explanation of the importance of the word. For example, you could write "Joseph McCoy built the first stockyards in Abilene, Kansas, in 1867. This was the beginning of the Cattle Kingdom and cattle drives." Be sure your sentences fit with your drawing.

Step 4　One student from the group should make a cover sheet for the lexicon. Another student should make a Table of Contents. In the Table of Contents, there should be one line for each letter. It should state the name of the page, for example, *A is for Abilene*, the name of the student responsible for the page, and the page number. When the lexicon is finished, your group can display it for others to enjoy.

Chapter Test 17

Part One: Test Your Understanding

DIRECTIONS: *Circle the letter of the best answer.*

1. Americans became interested in Alaska
- **A.** as a good place to grow cotton.
- **B.** after gold was discovered there.
- **C.** until they realized that it had few natural resources.
- **D.** because it was so close to Germany.

2. Which of these Americans gained control of the land and trade in Hawaii?
- **A.** missionaries and sugar planters
- **B.** tobacco planters and cotton planters
- **C.** sea captains and merchants
- **D.** owners of fishing and whaling ships

3. Which two areas gained by the United States in the Spanish-American War remain U.S. territories today?
- **A.** Guam and Cuba
- **B.** Puerto Rico and Guam
- **C.** Puerto Rico and the Philippines
- **D.** Cuba and the Philippines

4. President Theodore Roosevelt wanted the United States to use its power in the world because
- **A.** most countries around the world considered the United States to be weak.
- **B.** he wanted to fight in all the world's wars.
- **C.** he wanted to force other countries to buy only American-made goods.
- **D.** he believed that events in the rest of the world affected the United States.

5. Why did the United States want to build the Panama Canal?
- **A.** to move the navy out of the Caribbean Sea into the Pacific
- **B.** to fight in the Spanish-American War
- **C.** to link American territories in the Atlantic and Pacific
- **D.** to increase trade between Mexico and the United States

6. The main goals of the progressives were to
- **A.** improve government and make life better.
- **B.** end wars and make peace.
- **C.** stop immigration and foreign trade.
- **D.** help farmers learn new ways and grow new crops.

(continued)

7. Theodore Roosevelt called his program of progressive reforms the
    A. Square Deal.   **B.** Promise to People Policy.
    C. Government in Action Program.   **D.** United Way.

8. Governor Robert La Follette started a merit system in Wisconsin to
    A. reduce the number of hours in a workday from 16 to 14.
    B. make sure that children could be hired for any jobs they wanted.
    C. make sure that people who got government jobs were qualified for them.
    D. make sure that young people who graduated from high school could read
        and write.

9. The goal of the National Association for the Advancement of Colored People was to
    A. help unions win the right to strike.
    B. achieve full civil rights for African Americans.
    C. stop the railroads from charging high fares.
    D. stop immigrants from coming to the United States.

10. Why did the United States enter World War I?
    A. Russia asked for its help.
    B. France started killing American soldiers.
    C. The Turkish navy sank the battleship *Maine.*
    D. German submarines sank American ships.

11. The most feared of the new weapons used in World War I was
    A. barbed wire.   **B.** poison gas.
    C. the machine gun.   **D.** the handgun.

12. How did women contribute to the war effort in World War I?
    A. They helped men fight in the trenches in France.
    B. They were drafted into the army and navy.
    C. They flew airplanes in battles over France.
    D. They took over the jobs left by men going to war.

13. American women won the right to vote with the passage of the
    A. Thirteenth Amendment.   **B.** Nineteenth Amendment.
    C. Fourteenth Amendment.   **D.** Tenth Amendment.

14. The members of Congress voted **not** to join the League of Nations because
    A. they wanted the United States to stay out of other countries' problems.
    B. the League refused to elect an American to head the organization.
    C. the League wanted the United States to pay for the organization.
    D. they believed that wars were the only way to win new territories.

(continued)

Part Two: Test Your Skills

DIRECTIONS: *On May 7, 1915, a German U-boat sank the British passenger ship Lusitania. Americans were outraged, accusing the Germans of "piracy on the high seas." Germans defended the action, saying that the Lusitania was traveling in a war zone and that the ship was carrying weapons to help the British war effort. Leaders on both sides used propaganda to try to gain support for their cause. Read the quotation below by Germany's Baron von Schwarzenstein, and then read the statements that follow. Circle T if the statement is true and F if the statement is false.*

> In the case of the Lusitania *the German Ambassador even further warned Americans through the great American newspapers against taking passage thereon. Does a pirate act thus? . . . Nobody regrets more sincerely than we Germans the hard necessity of sending to their deaths hundreds of men. Yet the sinking was a justifiable act of war. . . . The scene of war is no golf links, the ships of belligerent powers no pleasure places. . . . We have sympathy with the victims and their relatives, of course, but did we hear anything about sympathy . . . when England adopted her diabolical plan of starving a great nation?*

T   F   **15.** Baron von Schwarzenstein claimed that the sinking of the *Lusitania* was an act of war.

T   F   **16.** Both facts and opinions are presented in the baron's statement.

T   F   **17.** The statement was meant to convince people that Germany should not have attacked a passenger ship even though it was in a war zone.

T   F   **18.** The baron said that Germans had no sympathy for the victims or their relatives.

T   F   **19.** The baron accused Britain of trying to starve the people of Germany.

T   F   **20.** Baron von Schwarzenstein's statement is propaganda.

(continued)

Part Three: Apply What You Have Learned

DIRECTIONS: *Complete each of the following activities.*

21. **Participants in World War I**
Identify the two sides that fought each other in World War I. Then list the countries that first made up each alliance.

a. _____ Powers   f. _____ Powers

b. _____   g. _____

c. _____   h. _____

d. _____   i. _____

e. _____   j. _____

22. **Essay**
Write a one-paragraph essay explaining how the progressives used the power of the federal government to make life better for Americans. Be sure to include the law or the name of the government agency involved.

NAME _____ DATE _____

Chapter Test 18

Part One: Test Your Understanding

DIRECTIONS: *Circle the letter of the best answer.*

1. Henry Ford found that he could produce cars less expensively by
    A. using plastic instead of steel for some car parts.
    B. hiring only immigrants to work in his factory.
    C. using a moving assembly line.
    D. using designs made in Japan.

2. Jazz developed from the musical heritage of
    A. Native Americans.   **B.** rock and roll.
    C. German immigrants.   **D.** African Americans.

3. What was the Harlem Renaissance?
    A. a system whereby people could pay a little money each month for consumer goods
    B. a program for rebuilding large areas of New York City after a fire
    C. the migration of African Americans from the North to the South during the 1920s
    D. a time of interest and activity in the arts among African American writers, musicians, and artists

4. The stock market crash of 1929 occurred because
    A. there were too many people without full-time jobs.
    B. more people wanted to sell stock than wanted to buy stock.
    C. farmers could not produce enough food for the country.
    D. World War I caused the economy to crash.

5. After the stock market crashed, many banks had to close because
    A. bankers had used bank money to invest in Roosevelt's Alphabet Soup.
    B. large numbers of people took their saved money out of banks in order to live.
    C. the government needed the banks' money to run its many programs.
    D. the government ordered them to do so.

6. How did the New Deal affect the federal government?
    A. The federal government lost power to the state governments.
    B. The New Deal let the President take the country to war.
    C. The federal government got more authority and more workers.
    D. The New Deal stopped government control over the railroads.

(continued)

NAME _____ DATE _____

7. The Works Progress Administration hired workers to
    A. take the place of union members who were on strike.
    B. invest government money in the stock market.
    C. take over the banks that had been closed.
    D. build roads, airports, and public buildings.

8. The building of hydroelectric dams helped economic development by
    A. allowing the government to sell electricity at low rates.
    B. allowing farmers to sell water at high rates.
    C. giving investors the opportunity to buy shares of stock in the dams.
    D. giving farmers more land on which to grow crops.

9. As the ruler of Germany, Adolf Hitler
    A. attacked United States naval bases in Hawaii.
    B. put only Jewish people into positions of leadership.
    C. caused the German stock market to crash.
    D. rebuilt Germany's economy by preparing for another war.

10. World War II began in Europe when
    A. Italy took over Ethiopia.   **B.** Japan invaded Manchuria.
    C. Germany invaded Poland.   **D.** Germany attacked France.

11. The United States entered World War II the day after
    A. Britain declared war on Germany.
    B. Russia invaded Britain.
    C. the Japanese bombed Pearl Harbor.
    D. the Germans attacked New York City.

12. How did the United States government make sure there were enough supplies to send to soldiers overseas?
    A. by closing many grocery stores   **B.** by rationing
    C. by helping farmers   **D.** by raising prices

13. During World War II, the United States government set up relocation camps for
    A. Native Americans.   **B.** German Americans.
    C. African Americans.   **D.** Japanese Americans.

14. What was the Holocaust?
    A. the German invasion and bombing of Poland
    B. Hitler's mass murder of European Jews
    C. German plans in World War II to invade eastern Europe
    D. the destruction of German cities by firebombs

(continued)

Part Two: Test Your Skills

DIRECTIONS: *Use the information in the time lines to answer the following questions.*

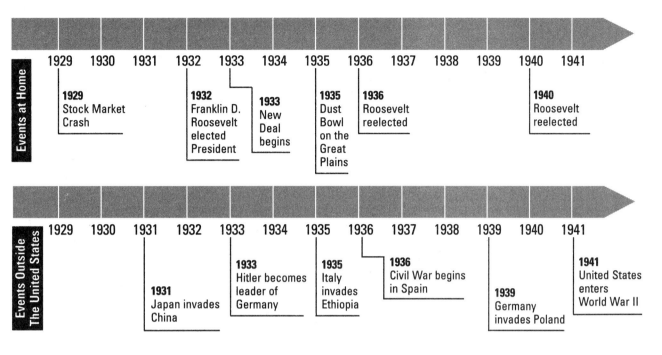

15. What was happening outside the United States at the same time as the Dust Bowl on the Great Plains?

_____

16. Did the United States enter World War II before or after the New Deal began?

_____

17. Was Franklin Roosevelt elected to office before or after Japan invaded China?

_____

18. Which event took place first—the stock market crash or the invasion of Poland?

_____

(continued)

NAME _____ DATE _____

Part Three: Apply What You Have Learned

DIRECTIONS: *Complete each of the following activities.*

19. *Economic Relationships*
    Explain the relationships among consumer goods, advertisements, and
    installment buying by defining the terms in the chart below.

CONSUMER GOODS	ADVERTISEMENTS	INSTALLMENT BUYING

20. *Which One Does Not Belong?*
    In each of the groups of words below, there is one word or phrase that
    does not belong. Circle that word or phrase, and give a brief explanation
    as to why it does not belong with the others.

    a. front   island-hopping   relocation camps

    _____

    _____

    b. rationing   free world   communism

    _____

    _____

    c. Harlem Renaissance   jazz   minimum wage

    _____

    _____

21. *Essay*
    Write a one-paragraph essay explaining why the Cold War developed.

Unit 9 Test

Part One: Test Your Understanding

DIRECTIONS: *Circle the letter of the best answer.*

1. Which of the following events led the United States into a war with Spain?
   A. the American attack on Manila
   B. the Spanish attack on Miami, Florida
   C. the sinking of the battleship *Maine*
   D. the firing on Fort Sumter

2. The Panama Canal is important to world trade because
   A. it links the Indian Ocean with the Caribbean Sea.
   B. it is the only body of water in the world large enough for cargo ships to travel on.
   C. it connects the Mississippi River to the Pacific Ocean.
   D. it provides a shortcut between the Atlantic and Pacific oceans.

3. President Theodore Roosevelt promoted the conservation of natural resources by
   A. making it illegal for hunters to shoot animals for sport.
   B. passing strong laws against pollution.
   C. forcing manufacturers to pay heavy fines for the use of raw materials.
   D. setting aside land for national parks and wilderness areas.

4. What was the purpose of Governor Robert La Follette's merit system?
   A. to give the government control over the meat industry
   B. to give government jobs only to people who were qualified
   C. to stop businesses from charging prices that were too high
   D. to stop strikes by workers' unions

5. What organization was formed in 1909 by W. E. B. Du Bois and other leaders to help African Americans?
   A. Interstate Commerce Commission
   B. Urban League
   C. Hull House
   D. National Association for the Advancement of Colored People

(continued)

6. During World War I, Russia, France, Italy, Britain, and the United States fought against the
    A. Allied Powers.
    B. Central Powers.
    C. Communist Powers.
    D. Axis Powers.

7. In World War I soldiers fought one another
    A. in tanks.
    B. in submarines.
    C. from ditches dug in the ground.
    D. with propaganda.

8. As a result of Charles Lindbergh's flight across the Atlantic Ocean,
    A. U.S. military leaders decided to use airplanes in World War I.
    B. people became more interested in air travel.
    C. the price of airplanes decreased.
    D. the Wright brothers decided to buy Lindbergh's airplane designs.

9. An important poet in the Harlem Renaissance was
    A. Carrie Chapman Catt.
    B. W. E. B. Du Bois.
    C. D. W. Griffith.
    D. Langston Hughes.

10. When the banks failed and Americans lost their money,
    A. people bought fewer goods and factory workers lost their jobs.
    B. people in France and Britain sent donations of food and money.
    C. only people who had invested in the stock market could pay for food.
    D. the government gave all homeless people free houses.

11. How did the New Deal affect the power and size of the federal government?
    A. The power and size of the federal government increased.
    B. The states gained more power than the federal government.
    C. Workers were able to take power away from the federal government by forming unions.
    D. The federal government became smaller but more powerful.

(continued)

12. After World War I, the countries of Germany, the Soviet Union, Spain, Italy, and Japan
    A. paid Britain and France for the costs of the war.
    B. were ruled by dictators.
    C. voted to become democratic countries.
    D. started the Cold War.

13. The United States entered World War II
    A. when Germany invaded Poland.
    B. when the United States started island-hopping.
    C. after Japan bombed Pearl Harbor.
    D. before the Philippines attacked Japan.

14. What caused Japan to surrender at the end of World War II?
    A. The Japanese army was trapped on Iwo Jima.
    B. Allied armies invaded the Japanese islands.
    C. The United States dropped two atomic bombs on Japan.
    D. Germany stopped giving the Japanese any aid.

(continued)

Part Two: Test Your Skills

DIRECTIONS: *Use the two maps below to answer the questions that follow.*

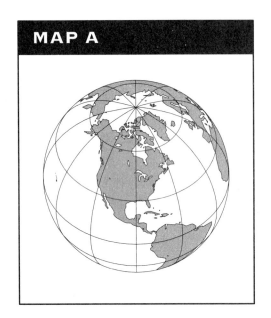

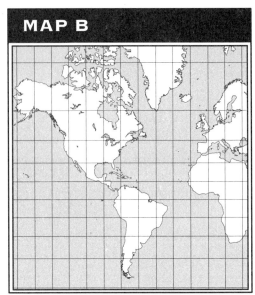

15. On which map are the meridians spaced equally? _____

16. On which map are the parallels spaced equally? _____

17. On which map do meridians get closer at the pole? _____

18. On which part of the maps do the land shapes appear the same?

_____

19. On which part of the maps are the land shapes the most different?

_____

20. Which map shows direction more accurately?

_____

(continued)

Part Three: Apply What You Have Learned

DIRECTIONS: *Complete each of the following activities.*

21. *Popular Entertainment*

List two new forms of entertainment that became popular in the 1920s.

_____

_____

22. *Participants in World War II*

During World War II, the Axis Powers fought against the Allies. List the countries that made up each side in the war.

Axis Powers	Allies
a. _____	d. _____
b. _____	e. _____
c. _____	f. _____

23. *Essay*

Theodore Roosevelt and Franklin D. Roosevelt both served as President of the United States. Write a one-paragraph essay describing the reforms made by these two Presidents while in office.

NAME _____ DATE _____

Individual Performance Task
Graph It!

In this activity you will use the facts at the right to make a line graph about unemployment in the United States. Then you will use your graph to answer some questions.

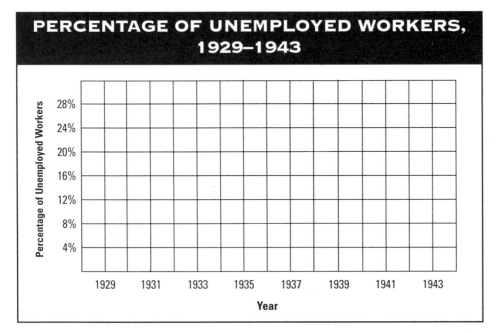

PERCENTAGE OF UNEMPLOYED WORKERS, 1929–1943

Year	Percentage
1929	3%
1931	16%
1933	25%
1935	20%
1937	14%
1939	17%
1941	10%
1943	2%

1. What effect did the stock market crash have on unemployment in the United States?

_____

2. What effect did the New Deal have on unemployment in the United States?

_____

3. What effect did World War II have on unemployment in the United States?

_____

Group Performance Task
Billboard Advertising

A billboard along a highway or street is designed to advertise a product, a service, or a cause to the people passing by. Most people have only 10 to 15 seconds to read a billboard. In this task your group will design and make a mural-size billboard that might have been used in World War II.

Step 1 Each person in your group should do research on one of the following billboard ideas:
- a billboard to get men or women to join one branch of the military (The military branches in World War II were the Army, Army Air Corps, Navy, Marines, and Coast Guard. Each branch of the military had a special unit for women.)
- a billboard to support rationing
- a billboard encouraging security and secrecy
- a billboard on women in the workforce
- a billboard on buying bonds to finance the war

Step 2 As a group, select the topic you want to use for the billboard.

Step 3 As a group, decide what words and pictures will be on your billboard. Remember that you must get your message across in a very brief period of time. Look at billboards in your area to see how they use just a few words to get their messages across.

Step 4 Make a rough sketch of your mural-size billboard. Then use watercolors or markers to make a final copy. Display your billboard where others can see it.

Chapter Test 19

Part One: Test Your Understanding

DIRECTIONS: *Use the words or names from the box below to complete the sentences that follow.*

airlift	César Chávez	Cold War
hawks	inflation	integration
missiles	Richard M. Nixon	nonviolent
Rosa Parks	Ronald Reagan	segregation
South Vietnam	superpowers	

1. In the years after World War II, the United States and the Soviet Union became the

world's _____.

2. When the Soviet Union blocked supplies from getting to Berlin, the Allies used an

_____ to take food and fuel to the city.

3. The United States blockaded Cuba when the Soviet Union placed

_____ on the island.

4. In 1954 the Supreme Court ordered an end to _____ in
public schools.

5. The Montgomery, Alabama, bus boycott was started when _____
refused to give up her seat on a bus to a white man.

6. Marches and boycotts are examples of _____ protest to
bring about change.

(continued)

7. The bringing together of all races in education, jobs, and housing is called

_____.

8. _____ formed the United Farm Workers to win better wages and conditions for farm workers.

9. In the Vietnam War, the United States fought on the side of

_____.

10. The costs of the Vietnam War and the Great Society programs led to

_____ in the U.S. economy.

11. _____ were Americans who supported the Vietnam War at any cost.

12. _____ was the first United States President to resign from office.

13. In 1985 President _____ met with Soviet leader Mikhail Gorbachev to discuss the "cause of world peace."

14. When President George Bush referred to "a new world order," he meant a world

without the _____.

(continued)

Part Two: Test Your Skills

DIRECTIONS: *It is the duty of all United States citizens to act responsibly. Complete the following activities on citizenship.*

15. What are four things a student can do to be a responsible citizen?

_____

_____

_____

_____

16. Describe how civil rights leaders such as Dr. Martin Luther King, Jr. and Rosa Parks acted as responsible citizens to fight injustice.

_____

_____

_____

_____

(continued)

Part Three: Apply What You Have Learned

DIRECTIONS: *Complete each of the following activities.*

17. *Time Line*

Match the letters on the time line with the events from the list below. Place the correct letter in the space provided.

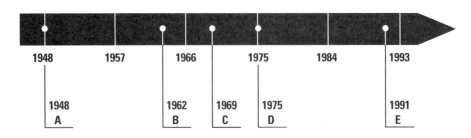

_____ breakup of the Soviet Union

_____ Berlin Airlift

_____ Cuban missile crisis

_____ *Apollo 11* mission to the moon

_____ Vietnam War ends

18. *Essay*

While he was President, Richard M. Nixon did much to ease Cold War tensions among the United States, China, and the Soviet Union. Write a one-paragraph essay explaining what President Nixon did to ease tensions.

NAME _____ DATE _____

Chapter Test 20

Part One: Test Your Understanding

DIRECTIONS: *Circle the letter of the best answer.*

1. The devaluation of Mexico's money in 1994 made it difficult for Mexico's middle class to
   A. vote in elections.
   B. buy consumer goods.
   C. communicate with people living outside Mexico.
   D. stage peaceful protests against the government.

2. The purpose of NAFTA is to
   A. increase trade among the United States, Canada, and Mexico.
   B. protect the cultures of the American Indians living in North America.
   C. place an embargo on imports into Canada.
   D. bring democracy to the countries of Central and South America.

3. In 1993 the people of Puerto Rico voted to
   A. declare independence from Britain.
   B. become a state of the United States.
   C. become a territory of Britain.
   D. remain a commonwealth of the United States.

4. Fidel Castro is the communist dictator of
   A. the Dominican Republic.   B. Cuba.
   C. Jamaica.   D. Brazil.

5. What is the purpose of the United States embargo on Cuba?
   A. It stops the United States from trading its goods with Cuba.
   B. It keeps the Soviet Union from sending missiles to Cuba.
   C. It prevents Cuba from holding free elections.
   D. It allows free trade to develop between Cuba and North America.

6. The United States military helped Jean-Bertrand Aristide return to power in 1994 as president of
   A. Bolivia.   B. Venezuela.
   C. Haiti.   D. Chile.

(continued)

7. Violeta Chamorro ended her country's communist government when she was elected president of

    A. El Salvador.   **B.** Nicaragua.

    C. Guatemala.   **D.** Mexico.

8. Deforestation is a major problem in

    A. Canada.   **B.** Cuba.

    C. Brazil.   **D.** Haiti.

9. The main purpose of the OAS is to settle disagreements

    A. between the free world and communist nations.

    B. among nations of the Western Hemisphere.

    C. among nations that fought in World War II.

    D. between the United States and Japan.

10. The Charter of Rights and Freedoms is

    A. an agreement to end communism in all South American countries.

    B. a bill of rights proposed by the Cuban people.

    C. the document that broke up the Soviet Union.

    D. a section that was added to Canada's Constitution of 1982.

11. What was the main effect of the Canadian Constitution of 1982?

    A. It caused a civil war in Canada.

    B. It divided the people of Canada.

    C. It led to closer relations with the government of Britain.

    D. It weakened the economy of Canada.

12. Which of the following Canadian provinces has objected most to the Constitution of 1982?

    A. Alberta   **B.** New Brunswick

    C. British Columbia   **D.** Quebec

13. Most people who live in Quebec, Canada, are

    A. Mexican Canadians.   **B.** British Canadians.

    C. French Canadians.   **D.** German Canadians.

14. People in Canada who are separatists want

    A. British Columbia to become a state in the United States.

    B. to end free trade between the United States and Canada.

    C. to limit French language and culture.

    D. Quebec to secede from Canada and become an independent nation.

(continued)

NAME _____ DATE _____

Part Two: Test Your Skills

DIRECTIONS: *Figure A below is a map showing the borders of countries in Central America. Figure B below is a cartogram showing the number of immigrants that came from each country to the United States. Use the information in the map and the cartogram to answer the questions that follow.*

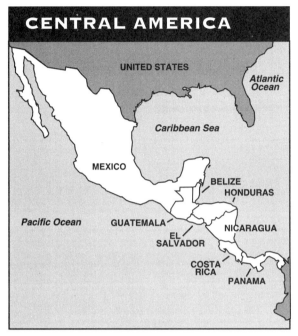

Figure A   Figure B

15. Which country sent the largest number of immigrants to the United States?

How can you tell? _____

16. Which country sent more immigrants to the United States—El Salvador or Belize?

How can you tell? _____

17. Which country sent the fewest immigrants to the United States? How can you tell?

_____

(continued)

Part Three: Apply What You Have Learned

DIRECTIONS: *Complete each of the following activities.*

18. Problems and Their Causes
Describe the cause of each of the problems listed below.

Problems of Nations in the Americas	Causes of Problems
the revolt of farmers in Chiapas, Mexico	
the conflict to restore democracy in Haiti	
the desire of people in Quebec, Canada, to secede	

19. Use Vocabulary
Match the term on the left with the correct description on the right.
Write the correct number in the space provided.

a. _____ deforestation

b. _____ interest rate

c. _____ province

d. _____ liberate

e. _____ metropolitan area

f. _____ commonwealth

g. _____ mestizo

1. a political region of Canada

2. a person of Indian and European background

3. a kind of territory

4. the widespread cutting down of forests

5. to set free

6. what a bank charges to borrow money

7. a city and all the suburbs around it

20. Essay
Write a one-paragraph essay describing the special relationship between the United States and Puerto Rico.

Unit 10 Test

Part One: Test Your Understanding

DIRECTIONS: *Circle the letter of the best answer.*

1. Which of the following United States Presidents ordered a naval blockade of Cuba during the Cuban missile crisis?
    A. Richard Nixon   **B.** John F. Kennedy
    C. Ronald Reagan   **D.** Jimmy Carter

2. What was the main goal of both the United States and the Soviet Union in the arms race?
    A. to control the entire world
    B. to bring an end to the Berlin crisis
    C. to have the most powerful weapons
    D. to start a war in Asia

3. Neil Armstrong was
    A. the first person to set foot on the moon.
    B. a U.S. military leader during the Vietnam War.
    C. the lawyer who argued for the desegregation of public schools.
    D. the first U.S. President to visit communist China.

4. Martin Luther King, Jr., thought that the best way to work for civil rights was to
    A. have a complete separation between white people and black people.
    B. use nonviolent protest.
    C. use any means necessary.
    D. organize a strike.

5. César Chávez started an organization to
    A. bring an end to the Vietnam War.
    B. win better wages and improve working conditions for farmworkers.
    C. work for the right of Indian tribes to run their own businesses and health and education programs.
    D. make sure that all jobs were open to both men and women.

6. President Lyndon Johnson's program to make life better for all Americans was called the
    A. Great Society.   **B.** New Horizon.
    C. Square Deal.   **D.** New Deal.

(continued)

7. Mikhail Gorbachev helped bring about change in the former Soviet Union through his policy of

    A. Québecois.   **B.** Nunavut.

    C. *perestroika.*   **D.** deforestation.

8. The fall of the Berlin Wall and the breakup of the Soviet Union led to

    A. the United States blockade of Cuba.

    B. the end of the Cold War.

    C. the growth of the middle class in Mexico.

    D. the resignation of President Jimmy Carter from office.

DIRECTIONS: *Match the description on the left with the term or name on the right. Then write the correct letter in the space provided.*

9. _____ Canadian province that wants to secede from Canada to protect its French culture

10. _____ free trade agreement between the United States, Canada, and Mexico

11. _____ amounts that banks charge customers to borrow money

12. _____ country in which Jean-Bertrand Aristide was elected president

13. _____ cities and all the suburbs and other population areas around them

14. _____ group that tries to settle problems between nations in the Western Hemisphere

    A. Haiti

    B. Organization of American States

    C. NAFTA

    D. metropolitan areas

    E. Quebec

    F. interest rates

(continued)

Part Two: Test Your Skills

DIRECTIONS: *Below are four political symbols of American history and politics. Explain what each symbol is and what it represents.*

Symbol   **Meaning**

15.

_____

_____

_____

_____

16.

_____

_____

_____

_____

17.

_____

_____

_____

_____

18.

_____

_____

_____

_____

(continued)

Part Three: Apply What You Have Learned

DIRECTIONS: **Complete each of the following activities.**

19. *Which One Does Not Belong?*

Listed below are groups of terms or names. Circle the one that does not belong in each group and explain why.

hawk	embargo	dove

_____

_____

commonwealth	Puerto Rico	Brazil

_____

_____

AIM	United Farm Workers	OAS

_____

_____

Fidel Castro	nonviolence	Martin Luther King, Jr.

_____

_____

(continued)

20. *Action*

Sometimes nations or peoples take strong action to achieve their goals. Listed below are three such actions. Explain the results of each.

Action	Results of the Action
a. Berlin blockade	
b. American blockade of Cuba during the Cuban missile crisis	
c. Mohawk Indians in Quebec, Canada, protested the building of a golf course on their land	

21. *Essay*

Write a one-paragraph essay explaining what caused the Korean War and what the outcome of the war was.

Individual Performance Task
Stamp It Out!

A postage stamp has a value stated in numbers, an illustration, and often the name of a country and a title or an explanation. In this task you will make a postage stamp (on an 8½-inch-by-11-inch sheet of paper) that honors one of the following people or events:

- the Berlin Airlift
- the end of the Cold War
- the actions of Rosa Parks
- the end of the Vietnam War
- the passage of NAFTA

Step 1 Select one of the topics above for the subject of a postage stamp or, with your teacher's approval, select a topic from this unit. Use materials in the textbook or do research in your school library to learn more about your topic.

Step 2 Make a rough sketch of a postage stamp. Show it to a classmate and ask whether it is clear and understandable.

Step 3 Make improvements in the rough sketch. Then make a final copy.

Step 4 Display the final copy of the postage stamp where others can see it.

Group Performance Task
Eyewitness News

In a television news story one or more reporters will talk to one or more people who have taken part in some event. The news story usually has an introduction, an interview with a person or persons, and a conclusion. In this task your group will prepare a news story as though it were to be broadcast on a television news program.

Step 1 Select one of the following topics for a news story or, with the approval of your teacher, select your own topic. Decide which role each member of the group will take.

Topic	Roles
Berlin Airlift	a reporter, a citizen of Berlin, and an Air Force pilot
Vietnam War	a reporter, two hawks, and two doves
Canadian separatists	a reporter, a person opposed to the separatists, and a person in favor of the separatists
Puerto Rico's relationship to the United States	a reporter, a person who wants Puerto Rico to be a state, a person who wants Puerto Rico to remain a commonwealth, and a person who wants Puerto Rico to be an independent country
the struggle for equal rights	a reporter, a person from AIM, a person from the United Farm Workers, and a person from NOW

Step 2 Use the textbook and library resources to learn more about your topic. The members of the group should try to find information that is close to what they would say if they were on a television news program.

Step 3 As a group, make a rough outline of the questions the reporter will ask and the answers that the others will give. Each person in the group will have specific things to say.

Step 4 Practice the news story. Time the story with a watch to determine how long it will take to present to the class. All members of the group should memorize what they are going to say.

Step 5 Have at least one complete dress rehearsal of the news story presentation.

Step 6 Present the news story to the rest of the class. Act as though you were on a live television program.

Answer Key

ANSWERS

Chapter Test 1

Part One: Test Your Understanding (4 points each)

DIRECTIONS: *Circle the letter of the best answer.*

1. During the last Ice Age, the oceans became shallower because
   A. the seawater evaporated.
   B. the ice in the glaciers started to melt.
   C. it did not rain for many years.
   (D.) much of the water was locked up in glaciers.

2. Beringia is the name of the land bridge that once connected
   A. North America and Turtle Island.
   B. Alaska and California.
   (C.) Asia and North America.
   D. Asia and Siberia.

3. Indian peoples tell of their beliefs about the world and their place in it through their
   (A.) origin stories.   B. theories.
   C. mesas.   D. technology.

4. People were able to keep a regular surplus of food after the development of
   A. earthworks.   **(B.)** agriculture.
   C. the atlatl.   D. culture.

5. The Olmec culture is known as the "mother civilization" of the Americas because
   A. Olmec farmers were the first farmers to grow corn in the Americas.
   B. the Olmecs built large earthwork mounds in their cities.
   C. the Olmecs were the first people to live in the Americas.
   (D.) Olmec culture influenced the cultures of so many later groups.

6. The people who built pueblos were the
   A. Olmecs.   B. Mississippians.
   (C.) Anasazi.   D. Hopewells.

(continued)

DIRECTIONS: *Fill in the blank with the correct word or words from the list below.*

adobe	agriculture	archaeologists
atlatl	band	clan
cultural diffusion	kitchen	kiva
nomads	tribes	

7. A small group of people who work together to do things, such as hunt, is called a ____**band**____.

8. People who wander from place to place and have no settled home are called ____**nomads**____.

9. Scientists who study the cultures of people who lived long ago are known as ____**archaeologists**____.

10. The ____**atlatl**____ was a tool used to throw a spear.

11. ____**Agriculture**____ developed when people began to plant and grow their own food.

12. ____**Cultural diffusion**____ takes place when people of different cultures begin to exchange ideas and goods.

13. ____**Adobe**____ is a kind of sandy clay that can be dried into bricks and used for building.

14. The ____**kiva**____ was a special underground room used by the Anasazi for their religious ceremonies.

(continued)

Part Two: Test Your Skills (24 points)

DIRECTIONS: *Use the information in the time line to answer the following questions.*

Beginning of Olmec culture along the Gulf of Mexico **1500 B.C.**
Beginning of Anasazi culture in the Southwest **100 B.C.**
Beginning of Mississippian culture **A.D. 800**
A.D. 1500

1000 B.C. **500 B.C.** Beginning of Adena culture in the Ohio River Valley
0 Birth of Christ
A.D. 500 **A.D. 1000** **A.D. 1300** Anasazi culture ends

15. Which of these took place before the birth of Christ—the beginning of the Anasazi culture or the beginning of the Mississippian culture?
    beginning of the Anasazi culture

16. The Hopewell culture developed in the area between the present-day states of New York and Kentucky around 300 B.C. If you were to place this event on the time line, would you place it before or after the birth of Christ?
    before

17. Which of these events took place after the birth of Christ—the beginning of the Olmec culture or the end of the Anasazi culture? **end of the Anasazi culture**

18. When was the end of the Anasazi culture? **A.D. 1300**

19. Which culture began at a time that was closer to the present—the Adenas or the Anasazi? **the Anasazi**

20. Which event took place earlier—the beginning of the Olmec culture or the birth of Christ? **the beginning of the Olmec culture**

(continued)

Part Three: Apply What You Have Learned

DIRECTIONS: *Complete each of the following activities.*

21. **Arrival Theories (4 points)**
    Archaeologists disagree as to when early people first arrived in the Americas. In the spaces below, give one argument that supports the Early Arrival Theory and one argument that supports the Late Arrival Theory.

EARLY ARRIVAL THEORY	LATE ARRIVAL THEORY
Possible responses: Artifacts have been found that are more than 12,000 years old; Beringia was uncovered from 45,000 to 75,000 years ago; cultural differences probably took longer than 12,000 years to develop.	Possible responses: Artifacts may have been caused by nature and not by humans; Beringia was uncovered 12,000 years ago; there is not enough evidence to support the Early Arrival Theory.

22. **The Development of Agriculture (6 points)**
    The development of agriculture resulted in many changes in the ways of life of early civilizations. Describe three of the changes in how people lived or how they made their living after agriculture was developed. Use one sentence for each change.

    Possible responses: Crops were developed; people stopped moving from place to place; villages became permanent; populations grew; jobs became specialized.

23. **Essay (10 points)**
    The cultures of the early Indian peoples were affected by the environment in which they lived. Write one paragraph explaining how changes in the weather and climate of their environments affected these early peoples.

    Possible response: The people depended on animals during the Ice Age for food and clothing. The uncovering of Beringia allowed people to migrate across Asia to present-day Alaska. The glaciers in present-day Canada melted and allowed people to migrate farther into the Americas. As the climate became drier and warmer and Ice Age animals began to disappear, early peoples found new ways to survive.

ANSWERS

Chapter Test 2

Part One: Test Your Understanding (4 points each)

DIRECTIONS: *Circle the letter of the best answer.*

1. The Indian peoples who got most of their food from the rivers and oceans close to their homes were the
   - **(A.)** Chinooks and Makahs.
   - B. Hopis and Navajos.
   - C. Iroquois and Cherokees.
   - D. Mayas and Aztecs.

2. Why did the Chinooks develop a special language?
   - A. They needed a language for their religious ceremonies.
   - B. They wanted to teach their children about their culture.
   - C. They wanted a language in which to tell their origin stories.
   - **(D.)** They needed a language to make trade easier.

3. The Makahs did **not** use parts of the whales
   - A. for food.
   - B. to make oil to burn as fuel.
   - C. to make ropes and bags.
   - **(D.)** to make totem poles.

4. Pueblo family members needed to store surplus food so they could
   - A. barter with wandering tribes.
   - **(B.)** eat when there was a drought.
   - C. feed the kachina dancers.
   - D. survive the long, cold winter.

5. How did the Iroquois stop the fighting among neighboring tribes?
   - A. They moved to the southwestern part of the United States.
   - B. They held a potlatch ceremony and invited all the tribes.
   - **(C.)** They formed a confederation.
   - D. They invited all the tribes to play a game of Little War.

6. The Indian people who adopted ideas from the Mayas and went on to build a large empire were the
   - **(A.)** Aztecs.   B. Anasazi.
   - C. Makahs.   D. Olmecs.

(continued)

DIRECTIONS: *Fill in the blank with the correct word or words from the list below.*

band	barter	buffalo
city-state	clan	confederation
kachinas	kitchen	kiva
slavery	totem pole	tribe

7. A _____ clan _____ is a group of families that are related to one another.

8. People went to the Dalles from all over the Northwest to exchange goods, or _____ barter _____.

9. The carved post that shows the history of a family is a _____ totem pole _____.

10. _____ Kachinas _____ are the guardian spirits of the Hopis.

11. The Plains Indians made clothes, tools, weapons, and food from the _____ buffalo _____ they hunted.

12. A _____ confederation _____ is a loose group of governments.

13. Each Mayan _____ city-state _____ had its own ruler and its own government.

14. Holding people against their will and making them carry out orders is called _____ slavery _____.

(continued)

Part Two: Test Your Skills (24 points)

DIRECTIONS: *Each group of sentences below has a cause and two effects. Place the correct letters in the spaces provided (C for Cause, E for Effect) to show which statement is the cause and which statements are the effects.*

15. **E** Northwest Coast Indians learned how to build canoes.

    C Northwest Coast Indians lived along the Pacific Ocean.

    E Northwest Coast Indians got most of their food from the sea.

16. **E** The Hopis filled a part of their homes with jars of corn and flour.

    E The Hopis used water from underground to water their crops.

    C The Hopis lived in an arid climate.

17. **E** Plains Indians hunted buffalo by following the buffalo herds.

    C Plains Indians needed a source of food.

    E Plains Indians made tepees that could be put up and taken down easily when the Indians hunted.

18. **E** The Aztecs built canals and paved roads to connect the islands in Lake Texcoco to the shore.

    C The Aztecs needed more land for farming.

    E The Aztecs built small islands in Lake Texcoco.

(continued)

Part Three: Apply What You Have Learned

DIRECTIONS: *Complete each of the following activities.*

19. **Indian Homes (10 points)**
    Match the descriptions of the Indian homes on the left with the names on the right. The names of the Indian groups that built the homes are in parentheses.

    C a house built partly over a hole dug in the ground — A. pueblo (Hopi)

    D a house made of elm bark with large doors at each end; home for several families — B. hogan (Navajo)

    B a cone-shaped house made of a log frame covered by mud or grass — C. pit house (Chinook)

    A an adobe building with rooms on top of and next to one another; home for many families — D. longhouse (Iroquois)

    E a cone-shaped house made of poles and covered with buffalo skins — E. tepee (Mandan)

20. **Essay (10 points)**
    Many of the early cultures and civilizations borrowed ideas or products of earlier peoples and made them better. The Mayas borrowed from the Olmecs, and the Navajos borrowed from the Hopis. Choose either the Mayas or the Navajos and tell what ideas or products they borrowed from earlier peoples.
    Possible responses:
    Mayas—stone buildings, large cities, social classes, and pyramids
    Navajos—baskets, pottery, weaving looms, tools, and crops

---

ANSWERS

Unit 1 Test

Part One: Test Your Understanding (4 points each)

DIRECTIONS: *Circle the letter of the best answer.*

1. The land bridge that once linked Asia and North America is called
   A. Adenas.
   C. Beringia.
   B. Siberia.
   D. Central America.

2. Which of these is used by Indian peoples to explain their beliefs about the world and their place in it?
   A. potlatches
   C. confederations
   B. longhouses
   D. origin stories

3. Each native group that settled in the Americas developed its own way of life, or
   A. kachina.
   C. diversity.
   B. legend.
   D. culture.

4. Which of these sentences about Clovis points is correct?
   A. Clovis points were used to make fires.
   B. Clovis points made hunting easier.
   C. A spear with a Clovis point could be thrown farther.
   D. Clovis points were useful in making pottery.

5. Making baskets, living in winter and summer camps, and hunting small animals such as deer, rabbit, and antelope are changes that took place
   A. before the land bridge linking Asia and North America was covered with water.
   B. before the atlatl was invented.
   C. while people lived near glaciers.
   D. after the giant Ice-Age mammals became extinct.

6. The most important crop grown in the Americas was
   A. corn.
   C. squash.
   B. wheat.
   D. beans.

7. The earthworks built by the Mound Builders were probably used for
   A. weapons.
   C. campgrounds.
   B. agricultural fields.
   D. religious purposes.

8. Early peoples exchanged ideas and products through
   A. specialization.
   C. trade.
   B. technology.
   D. shamans.

9. During a potlatch the Indians of the Northwest would
   A. give away gifts as a sign of their wealth.
   B. build pit houses for all the clan members.
   C. sing to a whale just before killing it.
   D. carve the history of their families on wooden posts.

10. How did the Hopis prepare for the possibility of drought?
   A. They built pueblos.
   B. They built large lakes to store water.
   C. They built special houses in the mountains.
   D. They stored surplus food.

11. Which of the following activities did the Navajos learn from the Hopis?
   A. hunting and gathering
   B. growing crops and weaving
   C. building canoes and houses
   D. making adobe and totem poles

12. What is the name for an adobe building that has many rooms built on top of and next to one another?
   A. hogan
   C. pit house
   B. pueblo
   D. kiva

(continued)

13. The Mandans made their shelters, moccasins, arrowheads, and blankets from
   A. the crops they grew.
   B. the fish they caught.
   C. the buffalo they hunted.
   D. the beavers they trapped.

14. The Iroquois formed a confederation because they wanted to
   A. move to the Northwest.
   B. develop a common trading language.
   C. build larger pueblos.
   D. put an end to the fighting among Indian tribes.

15. The Cherokees used plants in the forests for
   A. medicine.
   C. money.
   B. fishing.
   D. gifts.

16. The Mayas developed their civilization by borrowing and building on the ideas and achievements of the
   A. Hopis.
   C. Cherokees.
   B. Aztecs.
   D. Olmecs.

17. Which of the following was created by the Aztecs?
   A. tribe
   C. city-state
   B. clan
   D. empire

Part Two: Test Your Skills (18 Points)

DIRECTIONS: Use the map below to answer the following questions.

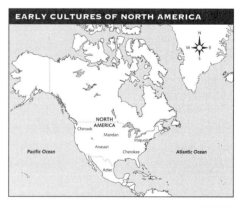

EARLY CULTURES OF NORTH AMERICA

18. The Anasazi lived in which direction from the Chinooks? **southeast**

19. In which direction would a group of Iroquois travel to visit a Cherokee tribe? **southwest**

20. Which tribe shown on this map lived the farthest south? **Aztecs**

(continued)

ANSWERS

Part Three: Apply What You Have Learned

DIRECTIONS: *Complete each of the following activities.*

21. *Indian Peoples and Technology (4 points)*

Technology is the use of scientific knowledge or tools to make or do something. In the following list, circle two items that are examples of technology. Then on the lines below, explain why they are examples of technology.

legend	theory	buffalo hide	(atlatl)
tribe	mesa	(Clovis point)	clan

The atlatl helped hunters throw their spears much farther.

The Clovis point made it easier for hunters to kill large animals.

22. *Essay (10 points)*

Water is an important resource for all peoples and can affect a people's way of life. Write one paragraph telling how water affected the Indian peoples of the Northwest Coast and one paragraph telling how it affected the Indian peoples of the Southwest.

Possible response: Indians of the Northwest Coast lived along the Pacific Ocean, so many of their activities involved water. They traveled on the water and got most of their food from the ocean. Indians of the Southwest continually faced a shortage of water. Drought, a constant problem, required them to store surplus food. They also had to use water from underground to water their crops.

Individual Performance Task
History Comic Strips

Comic strips have been included in daily newspapers for more than a hundred years, and comic books have been around for more than sixty years. Comic books and comic strips have focused on many subjects and themes.

A newspaper comic strip usually has
- a story or part of a story told in four scenes or "boxes."
- captions in some of the boxes, either above or below the scenes, that explain what is happening.
- "word balloons" that tell what the people in the scene are saying. Each word balloon points to the person who is speaking.

Create a four-box history comic strip about one of the peoples you read about in Chapter 1 or Chapter 2. In the comic strip, show how these people worked together to solve their problems or reach their goals. Give your comic strip a title that goes with the cooperative activity the people are doing.

Group Performance Task
Panel Discussion

All human activity is affected by the environments in which people live. The peoples you studied in Chapters 1 and 2 lived in many different environments. As a result, they had different lifeways.

In a panel discussion, two or more people will make presentations to the class. The people on the panel will speak about the same subject, but each will cover a different part of the subject.

In this activity the class will be divided into groups of four students. Each group will then choose a people studied in this unit and present a panel discussion about them to the class. Each panel discussion should last between 10 and 15 minutes. During the panel discussion, each person on the panel will cover one of the following topics:
- a description of the environment in which the people lived
- how the environment affected the kind of food they ate
- how the environment affected the kind of transportation they used
- how the environment affected the kind of housing they lived in

Each person on the panel should use the textbook or other resources to gather information for his or her part of the panel discussion. Panel members should each make one visual aid (chart or picture) that they can use to help explain their topic. One student should be chosen as the panel moderator. The moderator will introduce the subject of the discussion and will introduce each panel member before he or she speaks.

In planning a panel discussion (or any oral report), keep these things in mind:
- Know your information so you can tell it in your own words.
- Speak slowly and clearly so everyone can hear you.
- Look at your audience.
- Respect your classmates. Be a good listener when they are presenting their panel discussions.

ANSWERS

Chapter Test 3

Part One: Test Your Understanding (4 points each)

DIRECTIONS: Match the descriptions on the left with the names on the right. Then write the correct letter in the space provided.

__G__ 1. first European people known to have visited the Americas

__D__ 2. leader of first Europeans to visit the Americas

__H__ 3. name of the first European settlement in the Americas

__J__ 4. first European to make a globe

__M__ 5. European whose descriptions of the riches of China made traders want to go to Asia

__F__ 6. city captured by the Turks, closing off trade routes between Europe and Asia

__A__ 7. Portuguese leader who started a school for navigators

__N__ 8. Portuguese explorer who was the first European to sail around the southern tip of Africa

__I__ 9. Portuguese explorer who found a sea route to Asia by sailing around Africa

__L__ 10. local name for the island on which Columbus first landed

__B__ 11. Italian explorer who landed in present-day Newfoundland but told people he had found Cathay

__K__ 12. Italian explorer who figured out that Columbus had not reached Asia

__E__ 13. body of water reached by Spanish explorer Vasco Núñez de Balboa

__C__ 14. European who proved it was possible to reach Asia by sailing west from Europe

A. Prince Henry
B. Giovanni Caboto
C. Ferdinand Magellan
D. Leif Eriksson
E. Pacific Ocean
F. Constantinople
G. Vikings
H. Vinland
I. Vasco da Gama
J. Martin Behaim
K. Amerigo Vespucci
L. Guanahani
M. Marco Polo
N. Bartholomeu Dias

(continued)

Part Two: Test Your Skills (20 points)

DIRECTIONS: Read the problem below. Then use the information in Statements A through D to help you draw a conclusion that will answer the question in the box. Write your conclusion on the lines below, and tell how you reached that conclusion. Then list the letters of the statements that support your conclusion.

> **PROBLEM**—How could early explorers be sure that the Pacific Ocean and the Atlantic Ocean were two different bodies of water?

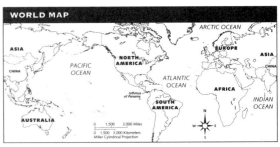

WORLD MAP

Statement A: Christopher Columbus tells the world he has found a new water route to Asia by sailing west from Europe. (1492)

Statement B: Giovanni Caboto announces he has sailed west from Europe to China. (1497)

Statement C: Vasco Núñez de Balboa crosses the Isthmus of Panama. (1513)

Statement D: Ferdinand Magellan sails his ship around the southern tip of South America. (1520)

15. Conclusion: Possible responses include: The Pacific Ocean and the Atlantic Ocean are two different bodies of water. The two later voyages proved that there was another ocean between the newly found continent and Asia.

16. Statements that support your conclusion: Statement C and Statement D

(continued)

Part Three: Apply What You Have Learned

DIRECTIONS: Complete each of the following activities.

17. **Changes in Europe (8 points)**
By the time the trade routes between Europe and Asia had been closed off, many changes had taken place in Europe. In the box below, list three changes in technology and one change in government that helped set the stage for European exploration.

TECHNOLOGY	GOVERNMENT
1. Possible responses: learned how to build faster ships;	1. Lands once ruled by warring nobles had become countries ruled by strong monarchs.
2. made a new kind of sail that allowed ships to sail against the wind;	
3. made a better compass	

18. **A Sequence of Events (6 points)**
The story of European exploration follows a sequence of events. Place the following events in their proper sequence by numbering them from 1 to 6, with 1 being the earliest event and 6 being the latest event.

__2__ The first European school for training sailors in navigation is set up.

__6__ One of Ferdinand Magellan's ships sails around the world.

__4__ Amerigo Vespucci concludes that Columbus did not reach Asia.

__3__ Christopher Columbus receives support from Spain to sail to Asia.

__1__ The trade routes between Europe and Asia are closed off.

__5__ Vasco Núñez de Balboa proves that Vespucci was right and that Columbus was wrong.

(continued)

19. **Essay (10 points)**
The first globe ever made in Europe was created by a German mapmaker who lived in Nuremberg, Germany. Although the globe was a remarkable creation, it had many things wrong with it. Write one paragraph explaining what was wrong with the globe.

Possible response:
The globe showed the Earth much smaller than it really is, which made it seem that sailing west from Europe to Asia would be easy. Also, the globe did not include the Americas, Australia, or Antarctica. In addition, it showed Africa too small and in the wrong shape.

ANSWERS

Chapter Test 4

Part One: Test Your Understanding (4 points each)

DIRECTIONS: Match the descriptions on the left with the names on the right. Then write the correct letter in the space provided.

__C__ **1.** Aztec leader when Europeans came to Mexico

__I__ **2.** leader of the Spanish conquistadors who conquered the Aztecs

__E__ **3.** Spanish conquistador who ordered his soldiers to kill the Inca emperor

__B__ **4.** leader of Incas killed by the Spanish

__L__ **5.** Spanish explorer who looked for the Fountain of Youth and named present-day Florida

__N__ **6.** Spanish explorer who heard stories about the Seven Cities of Gold and set out to find them

__G__ **7.** explorer who claimed for Spain all of what is today the southeastern United States

__M__ **8.** people who came to the Americas to convert native peoples to Christianity

__A__ **9.** peoples brought to the Americas against their will and forced to work for the colonists

__K__ **10.** explorer who looked for the Northwest Passage

__H__ **11.** explorer who founded Quebec and Montreal

__F__ **12.** European who founded a colony at Roanoke Island that soon disappeared

__J__ **13.** peoples who died from hunger, overwork, and diseases after being enslaved by the Spanish

__D__ **14.** Indian who taught the Pilgrims how to fish and plant crops that would do well

A. Africans

B. Atahuallpa

C. Motecuhzoma

D. Tisquantum

E. Francisco Pizarro

F. Sir Walter Raleigh

G. Hernando de Soto

H. Samuel de Champlain

I. Hernando Cortés

J. Indian peoples

K. Jacques Cartier

L. Juan Ponce de León

M. missionaries

N. Francisco Vásquez de Coronado

(continued)

Part Two: Test Your Skills (12 points)

DIRECTIONS: Use the information in the time line to answer the following questions.

15. Which colony started first—Roanoke or St. Augustine?

St. Augustine

16. How many years after Magellan's ship returned home did Drake sail around the world?

55 years

17. When did Hernando de Soto reach the Mississippi River?

1541

18. Which was started later—Plymouth or New Amsterdam?

New Amsterdam

19. When was the Plymouth colony founded? How many years was this after Elizabeth I became queen?

1620, 62 years

20. Where was the first English colony in North America? How many years was it until a second colony was set up by the English in North America?

Roanoke, 22 years

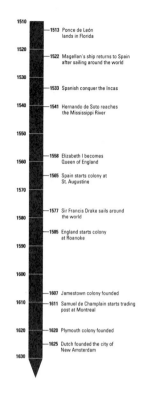

(continued)

Part Three: Apply What You Have Learned

DIRECTIONS: Complete each of the following activities.

21. Colonial Empires (16 points)

The colonies founded by Europeans in the Americas produced great wealth. In the chart below, list the areas where European countries had colonies and the source of profit for each country.

COUNTRY	AREA	SOURCE OF WEALTH
Spain	Middle and South America	gold, silver, crops
Holland	along the Hudson River, New Amsterdam	furs, trade
France	Canada, New France	furs, trade
England	eastern coast of North America	tobacco

22. Reasons for Coming to America (6 points)

Europeans had many reasons for setting up colonies in the Americas. Write in the chart the goal of each group listed.

GROUP	GOAL
French government	to gain wealth and power like the Spanish
Virginia Company	to make a profit for the company
Pilgrims	to find religious freedom

23. Essay (10 points)

There was both cooperation and conflict between the colonists and the Native Americans. Write one paragraph discussing ways in which colonists and Indians cooperated and one paragraph discussing ways in which they were in conflict.

Possible response:
The colonists and the Indians cooperated in many ways. For example, Indians were trading partners with the French and the Dutch in the fur trade. Chief Powhatan made peace with the Jamestown colonists, and his daughter married one of the colonists. Samoset welcomed the Pilgrims, and Tisquantum became the Pilgrims' interpreter and taught them what crops to plant. There were also many conflicts between Indians and colonists. The Aztecs and Incas were both conquered by the Spanish. A number of European explorers were killed by native peoples. The colonists building New Spain enslaved Indian peoples and forced them to work. There was much fighting between the Wampanoags and English colonists that arrived in Massachusetts after the Pilgrims.

(continued)

ANSWERS

Unit 2 Test

Part One: Test Your Understanding (4 points each)

DIRECTIONS: *Circle the letter of the best answer.*

1. The Viking settlement of Vinland was located in present-day
   - A. Iceland.
   - B. United States.
   - (C.) Canada.
   - D. Greenland.

2. One of the major problems with the globe made by Martin Behaim was that
   - A. there was no north direction.
   - B. the Atlantic Ocean was missing.
   - (C.) there were continents missing.
   - D. there were no longitude and latitude.

3. Marco Polo returned to Europe with stories about the riches of
   - (A.) China.
   - B. Plymouth.
   - C. Vinland.
   - D. Guanahani.

4. Europeans were eager to trade with Asia because they wanted
   - (A.) silk, spices, and gold.
   - B. wood, seashells, and silver.
   - C. clocks, mirrors, and beads.
   - D. vegetables, spices, and fruit.

5. Trade between Europe and Asia was stopped when the Turks captured
   - A. Roanoke.
   - B. Damascus.
   - C. Rome.
   - (D.) Constantinople.

6. Amerigo Vespucci used information he gathered from his voyages to conclude that
   - A. the Northwest Passage did not exist.
   - B. the Aztecs controlled the Seven Cities of Gold.
   - (C.) Christopher Columbus had not reached Asia.
   - D. the Vikings had not reached the Americas.

7. The explorer whose ship was the first to sail around the world was
   - A. Vasco Núñez de Balboa.
   - (B.) Ferdinand Magellan.
   - C. Christopher Columbus.
   - D. Juan Ponce de León.

(continued)

8. It was easy for Cortés and his soldiers to conquer the Aztecs because
   - A. the Aztecs had fought a civil war and were very weak.
   - B. the Aztec leaders could not be trusted.
   - C. the Aztecs lived in a land that had no physical barriers.
   - (D.) the Aztecs did not have guns or cannons.

9. The Spanish were able to conquer the Incas because
   - A. a strong earthquake destroyed the main Inca cities.
   - B. the Incas thought Pizarro was a god.
   - (C.) the Spanish killed Atahuallpa, the Inca leader.
   - D. the Incas had fewer soldiers than the Spanish.

10. The Spanish word for "conqueror" is
    - A. cartographer.
    - B. monarch.
    - (C.) conquistador.
    - D. navigator.

11. The Virginia Company of London sent colonists to Jamestown to
    - (A.) build a trading post.
    - B. work in the mines.
    - C. conquer the Olmecs.
    - D. find the Northwest Passage.

12. The main result of the fighting between the Hurons and the Iroquois for control of the fur trade was that
    - A. the supply of furs grew smaller and smaller.
    - (B.) the Europeans gained control of Indian land.
    - C. the Dutch were forced out of their colony of New Amsterdam.
    - D. they joined together to take control of the fur trade.

13. The idea of "no work, no food" as it applied to the Jamestown colony was stated by
    - (A.) John Smith.
    - B. Queen Elizabeth I.
    - C. Sir Walter Raleigh.
    - D. John Rolfe.

14. The main reason the Pilgrims came to the Americas was
    - A. to find gold and silver.
    - (B.) to gain religious freedom.
    - C. to set up colonies for the French government.
    - D. to take control of the fur trade.

(continued)

Part Two: Test Your Skills (24 points)

DIRECTIONS: *Use the map of South Carolina to answer the following questions.*

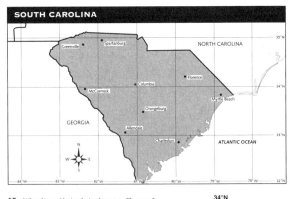

15. What line of latitude is closest to Florence? _____ **34°N**

16. What line of longitude is closest to Orangeburg? _____ **81°W**

17. What city is located near 33°N, 81°W? _____ **Allendale**

18. What city is located near 35°N, 82°W? _____ **Spartanburg**

19. What is the latitude and longitude for Columbia, South Carolina?
    _____ **34°N, 81°W**

20. Which city is closer to 83°W—Spartanburg or Greenville? _____ **Greenville**

(continued)

Part Three: Apply What You Have Learned

DIRECTIONS: *Complete each of the following activities.*

21. *Spanish Colonies and Labor (4 points)*
    The Spanish were able to gain control over large areas in the islands and on the mainland in the Americas. One of the first problems they faced was finding people to do the work in their new empire. Fill in the chart below about who did the work for the Spanish and how these people were treated.

What group of people did the Spanish first use as slaves to work on their plantations and in their mines?
Indian peoples

How were these people treated?
harshly; many Indians died from overwork, hunger, and disease

What was the second group of people the Spanish used as slaves to work on their plantations and in their mines?
Africans

How were these people treated?
the same as the enslaved Indians

(continued)

ANSWERS

22. The Mayflower Compact (6 points)

The Mayflower Compact was an important document in the history of the United States. Fill in the information about this document in the chart.

THE MAYFLOWER COMPACT	
What was this document?	a plan for self-government
Why was it written?	so Pilgrims could have laws to follow
Why is it important?	it was the first plan for self-government by colonists in the Americas

23. Essay (10 points)

Changes in Europe helped set the stage for European exploration. Write one paragraph discussing the changes in technology that encouraged Europeans to try to find a new route to Asia.

Possible response:
Europeans had learned how to build faster ships and make a sail that allowed their ships to sail against the wind. They also had made a better compass. These changes in technology helped set the stage for European exploration.

Individual Performance Task
A Traveler in the Americas

Marco Polo was 17 years old when he went with his father to China. When he came back 24 years later, he told many stories about what he had seen during his travels in China and all through Asia. Few people believed him when he told of his adventures.

Imagine that you are a world traveler like Marco Polo and you have visited the Americas. Your task is to write a story for your friends back in Europe about what you have seen in the Americas. Follow these steps in writing your story:

Step 1 Choose one of the following places to visit:
- Vinland
- the Caribbean
- Mexico
- Peru
- Florida
- Jamestown
- Plymouth

Step 2 Reread the section in the text that discusses the place you have chosen. You may also want to read other materials to gather more information about the place.

Step 3 Make an outline of the information you will include in your story. You may want to cover:
- animal life
- climate
- farming
- geography
- natural resources
- tools and weapons
- people (clothing, housing, language)

Step 4 Write a rough draft of your story. Review and revise your rough draft to be sure it has all the information you want to present.

Step 5 Have a classmate read your rough draft. Ask your classmate if anything is unclear or confusing.

Step 6 Revise and edit your draft, and make a final copy.

Group Performance Task
Make an Encounter Mural

Create a mural showing an encounter that took place when a European or a group of Europeans arrived in an area of the world new to them. You may use one of the encounters listed below for your mural, or you may wish to choose a different encounter.
- Marco Polo meets Kublai Khan.
- Christopher Columbus meets the people of Guanahani.
- Cortés meets Motecuhzoma.
- John Smith meets Pocahontas.
- Pilgrims meet Tisquantum.

Form a group with three or four of your classmates, and then follow these steps in making your mural:

Step 1 Choose an encounter and research it. Use the materials in the textbook as well as materials in the library. Make sure that your mural shows only what really happened.

Step 2 After you have done your research, choose a title for your mural and decide what will go into it. Be sure to create some written material to put next to your mural to explain to viewers what the mural is about.

Step 3 Make sketches in pencil on the mural paper. Then use paints, crayons, and markers to complete your mural.

ANSWERS

Chapter Test 5

Part One: Test Your Understanding (4 points each)

DIRECTIONS: Circle the letter of the best answer.

1. The Spanish government created the Spanish borderlands north of New Spain to
   A. establish an Indian farming area.
   B. make room for the horses brought from Spain.
   C. protect its gold and silver mines.
   D. protect its fur trade.

2. The Spanish built presidios to
   A. protect their navy.
   B. teach the Indians about Christianity.
   C. encourage cattle and sheep raising.
   D. protect settlers.

3. The oldest permanent European settlement in the United States is
   A. St. Augustine.   B. Jamestown.
   C. Plymouth.   D. New Orleans.

4. How did Spanish settlements in the borderlands change the lives of the Indians living there?
   A. The Indians learned how to farm.
   B. The Indians began to create origin stories.
   C. The Indians learned how to tame horses and raise sheep.
   D. The Indians began to build haciendas.

5. Life was hard for the Indians who lived at the Spanish missions because
   A. the Spanish refused to protect them from their enemies.
   B. they had to leave their families and friends.
   C. they had to give up their religious traditions.
   D. the Spanish would not give them any work to do.

6. Why did King Louis XIV make New France a royal colony?
   A. He wanted to rebuild his hold in North America after the fur trade was nearly destroyed.
   B. He wanted to force the Spanish to remove their presidios from New France.
   C. He wanted to raise taxes.
   D. He wanted to move to Montreal.

(continued)

7. When Jacques Marquette and Louis Joliet went looking for the Mississippi River, they hoped the river would help them find
   A. New Amsterdam.
   B. the Fountain of Youth.
   C. the Seven Cities of Gold.
   D. a route to Asia.

8. Who claimed the area known as Louisiana for the French?
   A. King Charles I
   B. William Penn
   C. Sieur de La Salle
   D. Count de Frontenac

9. In a proprietary colony the ownership belongs to
   A. the king.
   B. a company.
   C. one person.
   D. the settlers.

10. Which of these best explains why the Virginia Company of London founded the Jamestown colony?
    A. It was to be a trading post to make a profit for the company.
    B. It was to be a port for whaling ships.
    C. It was to be the first colony in California.
    D. It was to bring Christianity to the Indian tribes living in the area.

11. The most important cash crop in Virginia and Maryland was
    A. rice.   B. wheat.
    C. indigo.   D. tobacco.

12. The Puritans founded their colony in Massachusetts to
    A. search for gold.   B. make a profit from fishing.
    C. sell furs to New France. D. practice their religion.

13. The Connecticut colony adopted the Fundamental Orders, which was
    A. the first written system of government in North America.
    B. a set of guidelines for setting up the first school in North America.
    C. a promise to obey the orders of the British king.
    D. a plan to distribute indigo seeds to the other British colonies.

14. William Penn established Pennsylvania as a refuge for
    A. Indian peoples.   B. Jews.
    C. Catholics.   D. Quakers.

(continued)

Part Two: Test Your Skills (14 points)

DIRECTIONS: Use the information in the table to classify the colonies in three different ways. You may use abbreviations for the colonies when you write them in the charts below.

THE BRITISH COLONIES			
COLONY	DATE STARTED	TYPE OF GOVERNMENT	POPULATION (1770)
Connecticut (CT)	1635	Self-governing	183,881
Delaware (DE)	1638	Controlled by an owner	35,496
Georgia (GA)	1733	Controlled by the king	23,375
Maryland (MD)	1634	Controlled by an owner	202,612
Massachusetts (MA)	1620	Controlled by the king	235,308
New Hampshire (NH)	1623	Controlled by the king	62,396
New Jersey (NJ)	1664	Controlled by the king	117,431
New York (NY)	1613	Controlled by the king	162,920
North Carolina (NC)	1653	Controlled by the king	197,200
Pennsylvania (PA)	1681	Controlled by an owner	240,657
Rhode Island (RI)	1636	Self-governing	58,196
South Carolina (SC)	1670	Controlled by the king	124,244
Virginia (VA)	1607	Controlled by the king	447,016

Source: *Historical Statistics of the United States*, Vol. 2, Table Z1–19, page 1168.

DATE STARTED	
COLONIES STARTED BEFORE 1650	COLONIES STARTED AFTER 1650
15. CT, DE, MD, MA, NH, NY, RI, VA	16. GA, NJ, NC, PA, SC

TYPE OF GOVERNMENT		
CONTROLLED BY THE KING	CONTROLLED BY AN OWNER	SELF-GOVERNING
17. GA, MA, NH, NJ, NY, NC, SC, VA	18. DE, MD, PA	19. CT, RI

POPULATION	
LESS THAN 100,000	MORE THAN 200,000
20. DE, GA, NH, RI	21. MA, PA, VA

(continued)

Part Three: Apply What You Have Learned

DIRECTIONS: Complete each of the following activities.

22. **European Colonies in North America (20 points)**
    Spain, France, and England all built colonial empires in North America. Listed below are six items that relate to these empires. Put each item in the proper column, and write a short description of each. The first one has been done for you.
    • El Camino Real
    • charter
    • James Oglethorpe
    • John Law
    • portage
    • St. Augustine

    Possible responses:

SPAIN	FRANCE	ENGLAND
El Camino Real "the Royal Road" linked missions and presidios in the borderlands	a. **John Law** leader of Louisiana when it was a proprietary colony	b. **charter** official approval to take a certain action
c. **St. Augustine** oldest permanent European settlement in the United States	d. **portage** carrying canoes or boats around rapids or waterfalls	e. **James Oglethorpe** started the colony of Georgia

23. **Essay (10 points)**
    There were no plantations in Georgia before 1750. Explain why this was so, and explain why this changed after 1750.
    Possible response:
    Georgia's original charter did not allow traders to bring slaves to the colony. Because of this, Georgia had no plantations at first. After the law was changed in 1750 to allow slavery, the Georgia colonists set up plantations.

(continued)

ANSWERS

Chapter Test 6

Part One: Test Your Understanding (4 points each)

DIRECTIONS: Circle the letter of the best answer.

1. In most New England towns, the meetinghouse was used both
   A. as a jail and as a place of government.
   B. as a house of worship and as a place of government.
   C. as a house of worship and as a general store.
   D. as a general store and as a jail.

2. What was the purpose of a town meeting?
   A. to collect taxes for the king
   B. to educate boys and girls
   C. to have people work together to build wagons
   D. to make decisions about laws and town workers

3. How did market towns help farmers who lived near them?
   A. Market towns were a place where women, Africans, and Native Americans could vote.
   B. Farmers could trade their crops for goods and services.
   C. Every market town had a college where people could finish their education.
   D. British brokers visited these towns to buy tobacco.

4. The triangular trade route linked
   A. Britain, British colonies, and Africa.
   B. market towns, county seats, and plantations.
   C. British colonies, Asia, and Africa.
   D. colonial cities, market towns, and plantations.

5. Which of these economic activities contributed to the growth of cities along the Atlantic coast?
   A. whaling
   B. dairy farming
   C. growing tobacco
   D. growing indigo

6. Young people who lived in cities learned to do jobs that required special skills by
   A. going to college.
   B. becoming apprentices.
   C. traveling in Conestoga wagons.
   D. following the triangular trade route.

(continued)

CHAPTER 6 TEST   Assessment Program   51

7. In the southern colonies, most of the land was owned by
   A. brokers.
   B. church officials.
   C. planters.
   D. small farmers.

8. Early southern plantations were usually built
   A. along waterways.
   B. in cities.
   C. along major roads.
   D. near mountains.

9. What did southern plantation owners use instead of money?
   A. fish
   B. furs
   C. crops
   D. gold

10. Planters most often sold their farm products through
    A. British brokers.
    B. indentured servants.
    C. apprentices.
    D. constables.

11. Indentured servants
    A. were in charge of trade in the cities.
    B. always went willingly to the colonies.
    C. had to work for a set period of time without pay.
    D. agreed to work for a lifetime in trade for their children's freedom.

12. Wealthy planters were able to do the work required on large plantations with the help of
    A. British brokers.
    B. enslaved Native Americans.
    C. the local militia.
    D. enslaved Africans.

13. Which of the following best describes the education received by the daughters of southern planters?
    A. They learned science and math.
    B. They learned to read and sew.
    C. They went to college in Britain.
    D. They received no education.

14. The land between the Coastal Plain and the Appalachian Mountains is known as the
    A. heartland.
    B. fall line.
    C. backcountry.
    D. prairie.

15. Travel on the Great Wagon Road
    A. was very easy.
    B. was the only way to get wagons to the ocean.
    C. was important to the settlement of the backcountry.
    D. was one of the many roads that led to the backcountry.

(continued)

52   Assessment Program   CHAPTER 6 TEST

Part Two: Test Your Skills (15 points)

DIRECTIONS: Use the information on the product map to answer the following questions.

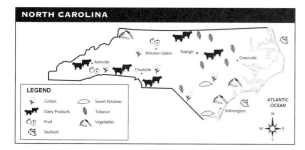

NORTH CAROLINA

LEGEND
Cotton
Dairy Products
Fruit
Seafood
Sweet Potatoes
Tobacco
Vegetables

ATLANTIC OCEAN

16. In what part of North Carolina would you find sweet potatoes as the major crop?
    the south

17. What is produced near Asheville? **dairy products, fruit, and cotton**

18. How can you tell that tobacco is the main farm product in North Carolina?
    There are more symbols for tobacco than for any other product.

19. In which North Carolina city would you find businesses involved with fishing and seafood? **Wilmington**

20. What is produced near Charlotte, North Carolina? **dairy products and cotton**

(continued)

CHAPTER 6 TEST   Assessment Program   53

Part Three: Apply What You Have Learned

DIRECTIONS: Complete each of the following activities.

21. **Water Transportation (5 points)**
    Transportation by water was very important in the British colonies. Listed below are five terms that are connected to water transportation. Explain how each term is related to water transportation.

    a. indentured servants   **Possible responses: traveled to America by ship**

    b. raw materials   **shipped from the colonies to Britain**

    c. slaves   **transported by ship from Africa to the colonies in North America**

    d. tobacco   **transported by ship to Britain to be sold**

    e. whale products   **hunters went to sea to kill whales and then returned to ports to sell whale products**

22. **Exports and Imports (10 points)**
    Exports and imports were an important part of the economies of the British colonies. In the chart below, list five exports and five imports of the British colonies.

EXPORTS	IMPORTS
a. Possible responses: dried fish, furs,	f. books, clothing, lace, machinery,
b. indigo, rice, tobacco, lumber	g. shoes, thread, tools
c.	h.
d.	i.
e.	j.

23. **Essay (10 points)**
    The running of a plantation required the participation of all the people living there. Write one paragraph about the jobs of the planter and the planter's wife.
    Possible responses:
    The planter had to see that the crops were planted, harvested, stored, and shipped to market. He also had to keep careful records of the business. The planter's wife had to clothe and feed her family. She also had to make sure that everyone living on the plantation had food, clothing, and medical care.

54   Assessment Program   CHAPTER 6 TEST

ANSWERS

Unit 3 Test

Part One: Test Your Understanding (4 points each)

DIRECTIONS: Circle the letter of the best answer.

1. St. Augustine was
- A. the main American port in the triangular trade route.
- B. the most important French mission in the British colonies.
- C. the main whaling port in New England.
- (D.) the first permanent European settlement in what is now the United States.

2. The Spanish government built roads linking Spanish missions to
- (A.) presidios.
- B. whaling centers.
- C. southern plantations.
- D. haciendas.

3. Which French explorers were convinced that they had found La Salle's river?
- A. Marquette and Joliet
- B. Cartier and Frontenac
- (C.) Iberville and Bienville
- D. Mongoulacha and Louisville

4. Which of these colonies was **not** founded for religious reasons?
- A. Plymouth
- (B.) Jamestown
- C. Massachusetts
- D. Maryland

5. Which of these areas in North America was made a proprietary colony by the king of France?
- A. Ontario
- B. Quebec
- (C.) Louisiana
- D. Florida

6. The town of Strawberry Banke, later to become the colony of New Hampshire, was started as
- A. a place to grow strawberries.
- B. a major trading post.
- C. a refuge for Quakers.
- (D.) a place to cut and ship lumber.

7. Decisions about the government in many New England towns were made by
- A. militias.
- B. proprietors.
- (C.) citizens at town meetings.
- D. British brokers.

(continued)

DIRECTIONS: *Match the descriptions on the left with the words on the right. Write the correct letter in the space provided.*

B **8.** a military fort built for the protection of settlers in the Spanish borderlands

E **9.** a small community of Catholic religious workers in the Spanish colonies

G **10.** a person who has been in prison for owing money

C **11.** a town's voluntary army

D **12.** a person who worked without pay to pay the cost of coming to the Americas

A **13.** a person paid to buy and sell things for someone else

F **14.** a place where slaves were bought and sold

H **15.** a place where the land drops sharply, causing rivers to form waterfalls

- A. broker
- B. presidio
- C. militia
- D. indentured servant
- E. mission
- F. auction
- G. debtor
- H. fall line

(continued)

Part Two: Test Your Skills (15 points)

DIRECTIONS: *The information in the circle graphs shows exports and imports in the British colonies. The graph on the left shows where the exports of the colonies came from. The graph on the right shows where the imports went. Use the information in the graphs and what you know from reading the unit to answer the following questions.*

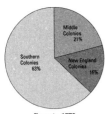

Exports, 1772

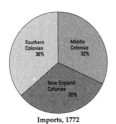

Imports, 1772

16. Which colonies had the most exports? What was the major product that was exported from these colonies?

southern colonies; tobacco

17. What percent of the exports came from the middle colonies? Why do you think these colonies had fewer exports than the southern colonies?

21%; The southern colonies produced and grew a greater variety and quantity of cash crops.

18. Which colonies had the most imports? Why do you think these colonies imported the most?

southern colonies; The southern colonies made money by selling their goods to Britain. The planters used this money to buy things and bring these items back to their plantations.

(continued)

Part Three: Apply What You Have Learned

DIRECTIONS: *Complete each of the following activities.*

19. *Triangular Trade Route* (15 points)

The triangular trade route was important to the economy of Britain and the British colonies. On the map below, draw the triangular trade route. On each side of the triangle, write the items that were carried by the ships on that part of the route.

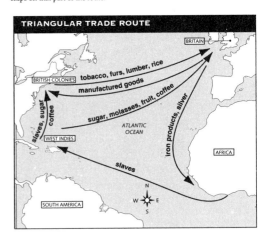

TRIANGULAR TRADE ROUTE

(continued)

ANSWERS

20. *Essay (10 points)*
The middle colonies attracted a wide diversity of European immigrants. Write a paragraph explaining why such a variety of people moved to the middle colonies.

Possible response:
William Penn established Pennsylvania as a refuge for Quakers. Because Penn's ideas about religious freedom extended to all religious faiths, people of many different backgrounds moved to the middle colonies.

Individual Performance Task
Imports and Exports

Trade was an important economic activity in the British colonies of North America. Listed below are some figures that show the value of imports and exports. Use the figures to make a bar graph. Your bar graph should show the value of both imports and exports from 1700 through 1750. The graph must have a title and labels.

After you finish making your bar graph, compare the values of imports with the values of exports. Write a list of trends you can see or conclusions you can make from your graph.

EXPORTS FROM NEW YORK TO BRITAIN AND IMPORTS TO NEW YORK FROM BRITAIN 1700–1750		
All figures are rounded to the nearest thousand. All amounts are given in pounds sterling. (The British unit of currency is the pound sterling.)		
Date	**Imports**	**Exports**
1700	49,000	18,000
1710	31,000	8,000
1720	37,000	17,000
1730	64,000	9,000
1740	119,000	21,000
1750	267,000	36,000

Possible responses:
- **The value of imports was greater than the value of exports from 1700 to 1750.**
- **The value of imports increased from 1700 to 1750.**
- **The value of exports increased from 1700 to 1750.**

Source: U.S. Department of Commerce, Bureau of the Census, *Historical Statistics of the United States from Colonial Times to 1970*, Volume 2, pages 1176–1177, Tables Z 217 and Z 218. Kraus International Publications, White Plains, New York.

UNIT 3 TEST

Assessment Program 59

60 Assessment Program

UNIT 3

Group Performance Task
A Radio Commercial

There was always a need for people to work in the British colonies in America. One way people in the colonies met their labor needs was by hiring indentured servants. Colonists would pay the cost of a worker's trip to America. In return, the person would work for that colonist for a set period of time without pay.

In this activity, the class will be divided into groups of five students each. Each group will create a radio commercial that would attract people in Britain to come to America as indentured servants. (Imagine that radio had been invented during the colonial period.)

In planning your radio commercial, keep these things in mind:
- The commercial should be 90 seconds long and should be recorded on an audiocassette.
- There must be a written script for the commercial.
- There must be at least five people in the commercial. You will need an announcer, a plantation owner, the wife of the plantation owner, a male indentured servant, and a female indentured servant.
- The commercial should give information about the benefits of coming to the colonies, the type of work to be done, and the number of years the person must work as an indentured servant. It should also describe the climate, food, recreational activities, and lifeways in the colony.
- The commercial can use background music and sound effects. You should be as creative as possible while remaining true to history.

UNIT 3

Assessment Program 61

ANSWER KEY

Assessment Program 187

ANSWERS

Chapter Test 7

Part One: Test Your Understanding (4 points each)

DIRECTIONS: *Fill in the blank with the correct word or name from the list below.*

Boston Tea Party	boycott	buyout
Committees of Correspondence	Concord	Crispus Attucks
French Canada	House of Burgesses	Loyalists
Minutemen	Parliament	quarter
repealed	representation	Sons of Liberty
tariff	taxes	

1. The British _____Parliament_____ made laws for all British people.

2. The first colonial legislature, called the _____House of Burgesses_____, was started in the Virginia colony.

3. After the French and Indian War, ___French Canada___ became a British colony.

4. American colonists were asked to pay for the cost of the French and Indian War by paying _____taxes_____.

5. The Sugar Act angered many colonists because it required them to pay a _____tariff_____, or tax, on goods brought into the colonies.

6. Colonists who supported the actions of the British government were known as Tories, or _____Loyalists_____.

7. Many colonists were against the Stamp Act because it was an example of taxation without ___representation___.

(continued)

8. Many colonists protested the Stamp Act with a _____boycott_____ of British goods.

9. Parliament _____repealed_____ the Stamp Act when it heard that nine of the colonies sent representatives to the Stamp Act Congress.

10. _____Crispus Attucks_____ was a runaway slave who was killed by British soldiers in the Boston Massacre.

11. The colonists formed the _____Committees of Correspondence_____ to keep colonists informed about protests against British laws.

12. The Sons of Liberty protested the tax on tea with an action that later became known as the _____Boston Tea Party_____.

13. Colonists in Massachusetts felt that to _____quarter_____, or provide housing for, British soldiers was intolerable.

14. _____Minutemen_____ were members of the Massachusetts militia who were always ready to defend the colony.

15. The fighting between the colonists and the British army that took place in the towns of Lexington and _____Concord_____ marked the beginning of the Revolutionary War.

(continued)

Part Two: Test Your Skills (20 points)

In the Spring of 1777, a soldier in the Continental army had an important decision to make. Should he continue to stay in the Continental army and serve with George Washington in the fight for American independence? Or should he return to his farm to plant crops so his family would have food for the next year?

In making his decision, this soldier had to determine the trade-offs (decide to do one thing and give up something else) and opportunity costs (what he would have to give up to get something else).

Fill in the chart below to explain the trade-offs and opportunity costs the soldier would have to consider to make his decision.

MAKING THE DECISION	
Trade-off in staying in the Continental army	Trade-off in going home to plant crops
16. a. Possible response: fight for independence for the country but may not have food for his family	b. Possible response: gain food for his family but may not gain independence
Opportunity cost of staying in the Continental army	Opportunity cost of going home to plant crops
17. a. Possible response: opportunity to plant crops that would feed his family, family may go hungry	b. Possible response: opportunity to fight for his country; Continental army may lose the war

(continued)

Part Three: Apply What You Have Learned

DIRECTIONS: *Complete each of the following activities.*

18. **Actions and Reactions (10 points)**
One action can lead to another. Listed below on the left are actions that happened in the colonies in the period before the Revolution. Fill in each box on the right with the reaction or reactions to that action.

ACTION	REACTION(S)
Britain wins the French and Indian War.	Possible responses: The British government decides that the colonists must pay for the cost of keeping British soldiers in North America. The British government will not let colonists settle in the western lands.
The British government passes the Stamp Act.	The colonists protest the Stamp Act, saying that it is taxation without representation. The colonists decide to boycott British goods.
The British government passes a tax on tea brought into the colonies.	The colonists boycott British tea. The colonists dump the British tea into Boston Harbor.
The Sons of Liberty, disguised as Indians, dump British tea into Boston Harbor.	The British government closes the port of Boston until the tea is paid for. The Royal Navy blockades Boston Harbor. Colonists are ordered to pay the costs of housing British soldiers.
British general hears that Patriot leaders and weapons are being hidden at Lexington and Concord.	Fighting occurs between British soldiers and colonists at Lexington and Concord. The Revolutionary War begins.

19. **Essay (10 points)**
After the end of the French and Indian War, Britain passed the Proclamation of 1763. Write one paragraph explaining what the Proclamation of 1763 was, why it was passed, and how the colonists reacted to it.

Possible response:
The Proclamation of 1763 was an order to the colonists to stop settling the western lands won in the war. Britain wanted to reserve these lands for the Native Americans so there would be no more wars. The colonists were angered by the proclamation because they wanted to settle these lands.

ANSWERS

Part One: Test Your Understanding (4 points each)

DIRECTIONS: Match the descriptions on the left with the words or names on the right. Write the correct letters in the spaces provided.

B 1. meeting of colonial leaders to deal with the British reaction to Lexington and Concord

H 2. letter sent by the Patriots to King George III, asking him to repeal the Intolerable Acts

I 3. person chosen to lead the Continental army because of his understanding of soldiers

F 4. soldiers hired by the British to help them in the Revolutionary War

N 5. person who wrote *Common Sense* and urged the colonies to break away from Britain

K 6. writer of the Declaration of Independence

M 7. religious group whose members are pacifists and refuse to take part in war

L 8. person who joined the North Carolina militia to fight at the Battle of Moores Creek

G 9. person whose poems supported independence

A 10. free African who fought at the Battle of Concord

O 11. Polish officer who came to America to fight with the Continental army

D 12. German soldier who helped train the Continental soldiers at Valley Forge

J 13. American victory in the Revolutionary War that led France to help the Patriots

C 14. battle that proved the Patriots had won the war

E 15. agreement between the British and the Americans at the end of the Revolutionary War

A. Peter Salem

B. Second Continental Congress

C. Battle of Yorktown

D. Friedrich von Steuben

E. Treaty of Paris

F. mercenaries

G. Phillis Wheatley

H. Olive Branch Petition

I. George Washington

J. Battle of Saratoga

K. Thomas Jefferson

L. Mary Slocumb

M. Quakers

N. Thomas Paine

O. Thaddeus Kosciuszko

(continued)

Part Two: Test Your Skills (12 points)

DIRECTIONS: Use the information in the cartoon to answer the following questions.

16. What is the man on the steps reading to the people? __The man is reading the__ Declaration of Independence.

17. What choice must the people in the cartoon make? __The people must choose to__ become Patriots and fight for independence or to remain loyal to the British king.

18. Why is this such an important choice for the people to make?
If the people choose to fight for independence, they must be prepared for a long war. If they choose to remain loyal to the British king, they must be willing to obey all the laws that the British government has forced on the colonies.

(continued)

Part Three: Apply What You Have Learned

DIRECTIONS: Complete each of the following activities.

19. The Declaration of Independence (12 points)
The Declaration of Independence was very carefully planned and written. It remains one of the nation's most important documents. In the chart below, describe the purpose of each of the four parts of this document.

FIRST PART	SECOND PART	THIRD PART	FOURTH PART
Possible responses: introduction that states why the Declaration was needed	lists the colonists' main ideas about government	lists the colonists' grievances against the British king and Parliament	explains that the colonies are no longer a part of Britain

(continued)

20. Events in the Revolutionary War (6 points)
Place the following events in their proper sequence by numbering them from 1 to 6, with 1 being the earliest event and 6 being the latest event.

5 American victory at the Battle of Yorktown

4 Continental army spends the winter at Valley Forge, Pennsylvania

6 Americans and British sign an agreement to end the war

1 Americans fight the British at the Battle of Bunker Hill

3 American victory over the British at the Battle of Saratoga

2 Second Continental Congress declares independence

21. Essay (10 points)
In the War for Independence, the British army had many advantages that the Continental army did not have. In a one-paragraph essay, compare and contrast the British army with the Continental army.

Possible response:
The British army was made up of professional soldiers who had the best training, the most experienced officers, and the newest weapons. It was a large army, with about 50,000 soldiers. The Continental army, on the other hand, usually had no more than 10,000 soldiers at any one time. The Continental army had never fought before as an army. Many had no uniforms, and they used whatever weapons they had on hand.

ANSWERS

Unit 4 Test

Part One: Test Your Understanding (4 points each)

DIRECTIONS: *Circle the letter of the best answer.*

1. The laws for the colonies were made
   - A. by the Continental army.
   - (C.) by colonial legislatures.
   - B. by royal governors.
   - D. by colonial women.

2. Which of these was a result of the French and Indian War?
   - A. The fur trade in North America stopped.
   - B. The French took control of four more colonies.
   - C. The Treaty of Paris was signed.
   - (D.) Parliament decided the colonists should pay for part of the cost of the war.

3. Many colonists were angered by the Stamp Act because
   - (A.) it was an example of taxation without representation.
   - B. there were no post offices in the colonies.
   - C. they were already paying for the tea that had been dumped into Boston Harbor.
   - D. the Loyalists did not have to buy the stamps.

4. Crispus Attucks was
   - A. the leader of the Stamp Act Congress.
   - (B.) the first person killed at the Boston Massacre.
   - C. a soldier who came from France to help the Continental army.
   - D. the most important Loyalist leader in the colonies.

5. What was the purpose of the Committees of Correspondence?
   - A. to punish the colonies because of the Boston Tea Party
   - B. to persuade colonists to become Loyalists
   - (C.) to pass news from colony to colony about protests against Britain
   - D. to try to get Parliament to repeal the Stamp Act

6. Which of these events took place **last**?
   - (A.) the meeting of the Continental Congress
   - B. the Boston Massacre
   - C. the Boston Tea Party
   - D. protests against the Stamp Act

7. Who made George Washington the leader of the Continental army?
   - A. the House of Burgesses
   - C. the Minutemen
   - B. the British Parliament
   - (D.) the Second Continental Congress
   (continued)

8. Which of these statements best describes the Continental army?
   - A. Its soldiers were mercenary soldiers.
   - B. Its soldiers were professional soldiers.
   - (C.) Most of its soldiers signed up for a year and then went home.
   - D. Most of its soldiers were well trained and had military experience.

9. *Common Sense*, a pamphlet urging the colonies to break away from Britain, was written by
   - A. Benjamin Franklin.
   - (C.) Thomas Paine.
   - B. George Washington.
   - D. George III.

10. Who wrote the Declaration of Independence?
    - A. Benjamin Franklin
    - (C.) Thomas Jefferson
    - B. George Washington
    - D. Thomas Paine

11. The writer of the Declaration of Independence included a list of the colonists' grievances in order to
    - (A.) show the unfair things the king and Parliament had done.
    - B. explain why the colonists were boycotting British tea.
    - C. apologize to the British king for the actions of the Patriots.
    - D. persuade Parliament to repeal the Stamp Act.

12. Which group of people refused to fight in the Revolutionary War because of their pacifist beliefs?
    - (A.) Quakers
    - C. mercenaries
    - B. Loyalists
    - D. Congregationalists

13. The enslaved Africans who enlisted in the Continental army
    - A. taught the Continentals how to fight.
    - B. supported the Loyalists.
    - (C.) were promised freedom after the war.
    - D. were all killed in the Boston Massacre.

14. The battle that convinced the French that the colonists could really defeat the British was
    - A. the Battle of Lexington.
    - C. the Boston Massacre.
    - B. the Battle of Yorktown.
    - (D.) the Battle of Saratoga.

15. The end of the Revolutionary War was marked by
    - A. the Battle of Saratoga.
    - B. the ringing of the Liberty Bell.
    - C. the surrender of General Cornwallis.
    - (D.) the signing of the Treaty of Paris.
    (continued)

Part Two: Test Your Skills (15 points)

DIRECTIONS: *Use the map of North America to answer the following questions.*

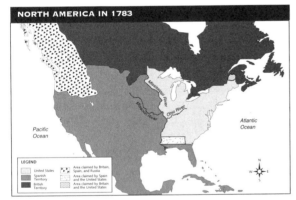

16. What two countries controlled the most land in North America?

    Spain and Britain

17. What countries claimed land that was also claimed by Russia?

    Spain and Britain

18. What countries claimed land that was also claimed by the United States?

    Britain and Spain

19. What two countries controlled land around the Great Lakes?

    Britain and the United States

20. What countries claimed land on the west coast of North America?

    Britain, Spain, and Russia
    (continued)

Part Three: Apply What You Have Learned

DIRECTIONS: *Complete each of the following activities.*

21. **Who Does Not Belong? (15 points)**
    Listed below are three groups of people. Circle the name of the person in each group who does not belong. Explain why that person does not belong.

WHO DOES NOT BELONG?	EXPLANATION
Paul Revere Crispus Attucks (Thomas Gage)	**Possible responses:** **Revere and Attucks were Patriots; Gage was a British general.**
Thomas Jefferson (George III) Thomas Paine	**Jefferson and Paine wrote about why the Americans should be free of Britain; George III was the British king.**
Benedict Arnold (George Washington) Charles Cornwallis	**Arnold and Cornwallis fought on the British side of the war; Washington was the Patriots' military leader.**

(continued)

ANSWERS

22. Essay (10 points)

The British army clearly had many advantages over the Continental army. Write one paragraph analyzing why the Continental army was able to defeat the powerful British army.

Possible response:
There are several reasons why the Continental army was able to defeat the British army. The Continental army fought the way the Native Americans did—in irregular lines and from hiding places. The Continentals were fighting in their own territory and for their own homes and freedom. The Continental army also received help from several other countries.

Individual Performance Task
A Letter Home

Your task is to choose a person who might have taken some part in the Revolutionary War and to write a letter from the point of view of that person.

First, choose one of the following persons:
- a soldier at Valley Forge writing home to his family
- the wife of a shoemaker, spending the winter at Valley Forge with her husband, writing home to their family
- a woman who is running the family farm writing to her husband in the Continental army
- a British soldier writing to his parents after the surrender at Yorktown
- a colonist who watched the Boston Tea Party, writing to a friend in Virginia

Then reread the information in the unit that is about your subject. You may also want to do research in the library to gather additional information. In writing your letter, be sure to include the following:
- events you, as the person writing the letter, have seen or taken part in
- problems you face, both small and large
- people you have met or heard about
- the feelings you have about the things that are happening

Be creative, but keep your letter true to history.

Group Performance Task
The Declaration of Independence

In the introduction to the Declaration of Independence, Thomas Jefferson explained why the Declaration was being written. The introduction is shown below.

> When in the Course of human events, it becomes necessary for one people to dissolve the political bands which have connected them with another, and to assume among the powers of the earth, the separate and equal station to which the Laws of Nature and of Nature's God entitle them, a decent respect to the opinions of mankind requires that they should declare the causes which impel them to the separation.

In this activity, the class will be divided into groups of five students. Each group will rewrite the introduction so that students in a lower grade can understand the reasons for the Declaration. Use dictionaries to find the meanings of the words you do not understand. Discuss in your group the best way to express the ideas in this opening paragraph.

After your group has rewritten the introduction, you may want to present it to students in another class to be sure that they can understand what you have written.

ANSWERS

Part One: Test Your Understanding (4 points each)

DIRECTIONS: Circle the letter of the best answer.

1. The Articles of Confederation and the Iroquois League were similar in that they both
   A. had a president.
   B. brought together different groups of people.
   C. stated people's desire to declare war on Britain.
   D. were headed by women.

2. A republic is a form of government in which
   A. the people are ruled by a king or queen.
   B. only the wealthy have rights and responsibilities.
   C. all people must pay taxes in order to vote.
   D. the people elect representatives to run the country.

3. Which of these was a part of the national government under the Articles of Confederation?
   A. a national legislature   B. a president
   C. a king   D. a national court system

4. Under the Articles of Confederation, Congress had the authority to
   A. raise a national army.
   B. make laws about taxes.
   C. print money.
   D. elect a single leader to run the government.

5. The purpose of the Northwest Ordinance was to
   A. prevent settlement in the Ohio River valley.
   B. set up a system by which new states could be formed.
   C. ask the states to send delegates to Philadelphia for a convention.
   D. end the troubles caused by Shays's Rebellion.

6. Which of these was a result of the Annapolis Convention of 1786?
   A. Each state started printing its own money.
   B. The Articles of Confederation were written.
   C. Congress created a new national army.
   D. Congress called the Constitutional Convention.

(continued)

7. The delegates to the Constitutional Convention met in
   A. Boston.   B. Annapolis.
   C. St. Augustine.   **D.** Philadelphia.

8. In a federal system of government, power and authority
   A. are given to the states.
   B. are shared by the national and state governments.
   C. belong only to the national government.
   D. belong to the people and the states.

9. The Three-fifths Compromise that was reached at the Constitutional Convention involved the
   A. number of British citizens allowed to live in the United States.
   B. number of houses of Congress to be created.
   C. counting of slaves for the purposes of representation and taxation.
   D. amount of power that was to be given to the national government.

10. Under the Constitution, how many senators does each state have?
    A. two   B. three
    C. four   D. five

11. Which of these is used to determine how many representatives a state will have in the House of Representatives?
    A. the amount the state pays in taxes
    B. the physical size of the state
    C. the number of government branches
    D. the population of the state

12. The branch of government responsible for carrying out the nation's laws is the
    A. executive branch.   B. electoral college.
    C. judicial branch.   D. legislative branch.

13. The Supreme Court is part of the
    A. legislative branch of the government.
    B. judicial branch of the government.
    C. electoral college.
    D. executive branch of the government.

14. Which of these helps to keep one branch of the government from gaining more power than the other two branches?
    A. the Three-fifths Compromise   B. the Preamble to the Constitution
    C. the system of checks and balances   D. the electoral college

(continued)

Part Two: Test Your Skills (24 points)

DIRECTIONS: Delegates at the Constitutional Convention often had trouble agreeing on issues. In order to write a Constitution, the delegates had to make compromises. In the spaces below are three issues related to the Constitution and opposing views on those issues. Describe the compromise that was reached on each issue.

REPRESENTATION IN CONGRESS

Virginia Plan: The number of representatives in Congress from each state would be based on state population.	**New Jersey Plan:** Each state would have the same number of representatives in Congress.

15. The Great Compromise

Possible response: Representation in the House would be based on the population of the states. Representation in the Senate would be the same for all states. All bills dealing with taxes would start in the House of Representatives.

COUNTING SLAVES

Northern Plan: Slaves would not be included in state population counts.	**Southern Plan:** Slaves would be included in state population counts.

16. The Three-fifths Compromise

Possible response: Three-fifths of all slaves living in a state would be counted for purposes of representation and taxation.

THE SLAVE TRADE

Northern Plan: The slave trade would be stopped.	**Southern Plan:** The slave trade would not be stopped.

17. The Compromise Over the Slave Trade

Possible response: Congress would be given the authority to make laws controlling trade but could not stop the slave trade for at least 20 years.

(continued)

Part Three: Apply What You Have Learned

DIRECTIONS: Complete each of the following activities.

18. Constitutional Authority (10 points)
According to the Constitution, some powers belong to the states, some powers belong to the national government, and some powers are shared by both the states and the national government. In the diagram, list two examples of each kind of power.
Possible responses:

Powers of the State Governments — Shared Powers — Powers of the National Government

19. Essay (10 points)
The delegates to the Constitutional Convention had to make compromises before they could finish writing the Constitution. One of the first compromises they made was the Great Compromise. In a one-paragraph essay, explain what this compromise was about and what its results were.

Possible response: The basic issue was the sharing of power between large and small states. Under this compromise, representation in the House of Representatives would be based on the population of each state. In the Senate each state would have two senators.

ANSWERS

Chapter Test 10

Part One: Test Your Understanding (4 points each)

DIRECTIONS: Circle the letter of the best answer.

1. *The Federalist* was a collection of letters that
   A. created rules for the new government.
   B. set up the method for electing the President.
   C. defended the Constitution.
   D. claimed there was no need for a bill of rights.

2. The First Amendment in the Bill of Rights
   A. protects religious freedom.
   B. creates the electoral college.
   C. gives people the right to have guns.
   D. lets each state have two senators.

3. The right to a fair, public trial with a lawyer is
   A. a check-and-balance power.
   B. due process of law.
   C. part of the federal system.
   D. a responsibility of citizenship.

4. According to the Ninth Amendment, all people have
   A. the right to serve on a jury.
   B. the right to refuse to pay taxes.
   C. basic human rights.
   D. the right to keep and bear arms.

5. President George Washington chose Thomas Jefferson to
   A. build a national army.
   B. advise him on matters of law.
   C. set up a new banking system.
   D. establish ties with leading world powers.

6. The attorney general is the
   A. President's legal adviser.
   B. leader of the army.
   C. leader of the House of Representatives.
   D. most important justice on the Supreme Court.

(continued)

7. Which of these best describes the ideas of Alexander Hamilton?
   A. He wanted most people to live on farms.
   B. He wanted to strengthen the authority of the states.
   C. He wanted close ties with France.
   D. He wanted a strong national government.

8. Members of the Democratic-Republican party supported
   A. John Adams.
   B. Alexander Hamilton.
   C. Thomas Jefferson.
   D. George Washington.

DIRECTIONS: Match the descriptions on the left with the words or names on the right. Write the correct letter in the space provided.

9. **F** people who wanted to ratify the Constitution

10. **C** people who agreed to ratify the Constitution only if it included a bill of rights

11. **G** protects the right of free speech

12. **A** protects people's homes from unreasonable government searches

13. **D** advisers to the President

14. **E** person whose ideas about government differed greatly from those of Alexander Hamilton

15. **B** first President to live in the White House

A. Fourth Amendment
B. John Adams
C. Anti-Federalists
D. Cabinet
E. Thomas Jefferson
F. Federalists
G. First Amendment

(continued)

Part Two: Test Your Skills (10 points)

DIRECTIONS: A book cover can be a document that gives information about a publication. Study the cover of The Federalist below and answer the questions that follow.

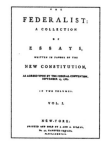

16. *The Federalist* is a collection of **essays** .

17. In what city was *The Federalist* published? **New York**

18. How many volumes of *The Federalist* were published? **two**

19. Does this document make you think many people were in favor of the Constitution? Explain your answer. **Answers should reflect that many people were probably in favor of ratifying the Constitution because a 2-volume collection of essays in favor of ratification was published.**

20. What do you think the reason was for publishing this collection of essays? **Possible responses may include that the writers wanted to show and encourage support for the Constitution so that it would be ratified by all states.**

(continued)

Part Three: Apply What You Have Learned

DIRECTIONS: Complete each of the following activities.

21. **Leaders of Government (10 points)**
Each of the individuals shown on the left did important work in the first government under the Constitution. Draw a line from each person's name to the position he held in the government.

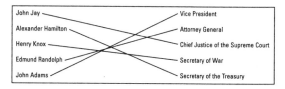

22. **Responsibilities of Citizenship (10 points)**
The Constitution lists the rights guaranteed to all Americans. The Constitution also suggests the responsibilities of citizenship. List five of these responsibilities.

   a. **Possible responses: obey the laws, vote in**
   b. **elections, defend the country, serve on a jury,**
   c. **pay taxes**
   d. _____
   e. _____

23. **Essay (10 points)**
On March 4, 1797, the second President of the United States took the oath of office. Write a paragraph telling who took the oath of office on that day and why that event marked an important day in history.
Possible response:
John Adams became the second President of the United States. This was an important day because it marked one of the first times in the history of the world that a nation had changed leaders in a peaceful election.

(continued)

ANSWERS

Unit 5 Test

Part One: Test Your Understanding (4 points each)

DIRECTIONS: *Circle the letter of the best answer.*

1. The Articles of Confederation limited the authority of Congress by
   A. giving more power to the President.
   B. weakening the power of the states.
   C. creating a republic.
   (D.) requiring 9 of 13 states to agree before a law is passed.

2. Shays's Rebellion showed people
   A. how to get a law passed by Congress.
   (B.) the weakness of government under the Articles of Confederation.
   C. the value of making compromises.
   D. why a bill of rights was needed.

3. Making the national government strong without taking away the powers of the states was an accomplishment of
   (A.) the Constitutional Convention.
   B. the Articles of Confederation.
   C. President Washington and his Cabinet.
   D. the Annapolis Convention.

4. In a federal system of government, power and authority
   A. belong to the President alone.
   B. belong to the national government alone.
   C. belong to the states alone.
   (D.) are shared by the states and the national government.

5. Who has the authority to veto a bill?
   (A.) the President   B. the Supreme Court
   C. the Senate   D. the Cabinet

6. The writers of the Constitution made sure no one branch of government could become too powerful by
   A. making the President the leader of all three branches.
   (B.) creating a system of checks and balances.
   C. creating political parties.
   D. appointing the leader of each branch for life.

(continued)

UNIT 5 TEST   Assessment Program 87

7. People who were Federalists
   A. supported a weak national government.
   B. wanted the Preamble to the Constitution to begin with "We the States. . . ."
   C. wanted a bill of rights added to the Constitution.
   (D.) wanted to ratify the Constitution.

8. Which of these was written by Alexander Hamilton, James Madison, and John Jay?
   A. the Articles of Confederation
   B. the Constitution of the United States
   (C.) *The Federalist*
   D. the Declaration of Independence

9. Freedom of religion, speech, and the press are protected by the
   (A.) First Amendment.   B. Second Amendment.
   C. Fifth Amendment.   D. Tenth Amendment.

10. Basic human rights are protected by the
    A. Second Amendment.   B. Third Amendment.
    (C.) Ninth Amendment.   D. Tenth Amendment.

11. To help him do the work of the executive branch, the first President of the United States created
    (A.) a Cabinet.   B. a federal system of government.
    C. the Supreme Court.   D. a two-house Congress.

12. Creating a strong national government was the goal of
    A. Thomas Jefferson.   (B.) Alexander Hamilton.
    C. James Madison.   D. Patrick Henry.

13. The first two political parties in the United States were
    A. the Democratic party and the Republican party.
    B. the Loyalist party and the Patriot party.
    (C.) the Democratic-Republican party and the Federalist party.
    D. the Tory party and the Loyalist party.

14. Which of these best describes the transfer of the presidency of George Washington to the presidency of John Adams?
    (A.) It was one of the first times that a nation had changed leaders by peaceful election.
    B. It was a victory for the Anti-Federalist party.
    C. It came at the end of George Washington's third term in office.
    D. It was the first election for President under the Constitution.

(continued)

88 Assessment Program   UNIT 5 TEST

Part Two: Test Your Skills (18 points)

DIRECTIONS: *Answer the questions by using your pencil or the edge of a ruler to measure distances on the map of the Mohawk Trail below.*

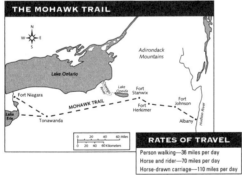

15. How far is it from Fort Niagara to Tonawanda? How long would it take for a person to travel from Fort Niagara to Tonawanda in a horse-drawn carriage?

    about 60 miles; about half a day

16. How long would it take for a person to go by horse from Fort Herkimer to Albany?

    about one day

17. How long would it take a person to walk from Tonawanda to Fort Stanwix? How long would it take by horse and rider? by horse-drawn carriage?

    about four days; about two days; about one and one-quarter of a day

(continued)

UNIT 5 TEST   Assessment Program 89

Part Three: Apply What You Have Learned

DIRECTIONS: *Complete each of the following activities.*

18. *The Three Branches of Government (9 points)*
    Fill in the missing information in the chart below.

LEGISLATIVE BRANCH	EXECUTIVE BRANCH	JUDICIAL BRANCH
Purpose: **make laws**	Purpose: **carry out laws**	Purpose: **decide whether laws are working fairly**
Two houses: **Senate and House of Representatives**	Leader: **President**	Leading body: **Supreme Court**
Number in each body today: **100 senators—2 per state 435 representatives—based on state population**	How selected: **Citizens vote for the electors; electors vote for the President**	How selected: **President appoints and Senate confirms**

(continued)

90 Assessment Program   UNIT 5 TEST

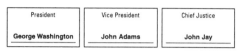

ANSWERS

19. *Government Under the Constitution (7 points)*
Fill in the names of the first United States government below.

President	Vice President	Chief Justice
George Washington	**John Adams**	**John Jay**

Secretary of State	Secretary of War	Secretary of the Treasury	Attorney General
Thomas Jefferson	**Henry Knox**	**Alexander Hamilton**	**Edmund Randolph**

20. *Essay (10 points)*
A bill must go through many steps before it becomes a law. Write a paragraph explaining how a bill becomes a law.
Possible response:
A member of the House of Representatives or the Senate introduces the bill. The bill is then reviewed by a committee. The House and Senate then vote to approve the bill. If the bill passes, it is sent to the President. If the President signs the bill, it becomes a law. If the President vetoes the bill, Congress can still make the bill a law by a two-thirds majority vote.

UNIT 5 TEST   Assessment Program 91

Individual Performance Task
Preamble to the United States Constitution

The words of the Preamble to the United States Constitution set forth the goals of the new government. Read the Preamble. Look up in a dictionary any words in the Preamble you do not understand. Discuss with your teacher and classmates the meaning of the Preamble.

> *We the people of the United States, in order to form a more perfect Union, establish justice, insure domestic tranquillity, provide for the common defense, promote the general welfare, and secure the blessings of liberty to ourselves and our posterity, do ordain and establish this Constitution for the United States of America . . .*

Today the national government carries out activities that are designed to fulfill the goals expressed in the Preamble. The basic goals of the government are:
- to form a more perfect union
- to establish justice
- to ensure domestic tranquillity
- to provide for the common defense
- to promote the general welfare
- to secure the blessings of liberty

Write the Preamble in the center of a sheet of art paper or posterboard. Make a collage showing four ways that the government carries out the goals of the Preamble. Use pictures from newspapers and magazines to show these activities, or draw your own pictures. Label each picture to show what goal mentioned in the Preamble is represented.

92 Assessment Program   UNIT 5

Group Performance Task
Create a One-Act Play

Use one of the following four topics as the basis for writing a one-act play. There should be between four and six actors in the play, and the play should take 10 to 15 minutes to perform. Gather information about your topic from your textbook, the school library, or both. Try to be both creative and historically accurate in your script.

Topic 1: Government Under the Articles of Confederation

Subject: Describe government under the Articles of Confederation, including its weaknesses and its strengths.
Characters: Narrator, John Dickinson, members of Congress, Daniel Shays, and Alexander Hamilton

Topic 2: The Great Compromise

Subject: Describe the ideas of the large states and of the small states at the Constitutional Convention. What did they want? What plans did they discuss? What was the Great Compromise? What did the large states get? What did the small states get?
Characters: George Washington as the narrator (president of the convention), delegates from the large states, and delegates from the small states

Topic 3: Ratifying the Constitution

Subject: Describe the debate over the ratification of the Constitution. Use the debate and the compromise over a bill of rights as the central point of your play.
Characters: Narrator, Federalists, and Anti-Federalists

Topic 4: The Bill of Rights

Subject: Describe at least five rights of American citizens that are protected by the Bill of Rights.
Characters: Narrator and individual citizens using their rights

UNIT 5   Assessment Program 93

ANSWER KEY   Assessment Program   **195**

ANSWERS

Chapter Test 11

Part One: Test Your Understanding (4 points each)

DIRECTIONS: Circle the letter of the best answer.

1. To make his way over the mountains into Kentucky, Daniel Boone first tried to find the
   A. Mississippi River. B. Louisiana Purchase.
   C. Warrior's Path. D. Northwest Passage.

2. When Daniel Boone first went to Kentucky, he found many
   A. wild horses. B. trading settlements.
   C. canals. **D. buffalo.**

3. What did Daniel Boone do to help settle the West?
   A. He helped make the Wilderness Road.
   B. He explored the Mississippi River.
   C. He traded goods with people in New Orleans.
   D. He signed a peace treaty with the Cherokees and the Shawnees.

4. One of the first things that pioneer families had to do when they moved to the western frontier was to
   A. build adobe houses. B. build missions.
   C. clear thick forests. D. set up a government.

5. To stop the United States frontier from moving farther west, Spain
   A. declared war on Tennessee.
   B. closed the port of New Orleans to western farmers.
   C. ordered the Indian tribes to stop trading with Americans.
   D. sent Spanish settlers into Kentucky.

6. How did the Louisiana Purchase change the United States?
   A. It cut the size of the United States in half.
   B. It outlawed slavery in all states east of Louisiana.
   C. It doubled the size of the country.
   D. It increased the number of states in the country to 14.

7. Which of the following people served as a guide for the Lewis and Clark expedition?
   A. Sacagawea B. Tecumseh
   C. the Prophet D. Cameahwait

(continued)

8. The Lewis and Clark expedition helped later pioneers by
   A. building the National Highway.
   B. mapping passes through the Rockies.
   C. finding a route to the Atlantic Ocean.
   D. clearing the Cumberland Gap.

9. Who wanted to form a strong confederation of Indians in Kentucky and Tennessee?
   A. Andrew Jackson B. William Henry Harrison
   C. Tecumseh D. Sequoyah

10. One result of the Battle of Tippecanoe was that
    A. the Americans and the Indians signed a peace treaty.
    B. the Indians agreed to leave the Northwest Territory.
    C. the Americans agreed to pay the Indians for the cost of the war.
    D. the Americans destroyed Prophetstown.

11. Which of the following groups of Americans did not want the United States to go to war with Britain in 1812?
    A. western farmers B. southern planters
    C. War Hawks **D. northern merchants**

12. Which of the following was a turning point in the War of 1812?
    A. the battle on Lake Erie
    B. the impressment of American sailors
    C. the formation of the War Hawks
    D. the Battle of New Orleans

13. After the War of 1812, during the Era of Good Feelings, the United States government
    A. was stronger in its dealings with foreign nations.
    B. sent people to explore land gained from France.
    C. was too weak to stop European countries from expanding their American empires.
    D. lost land to Spain and Britain.

14. Who wrote a poem about American bravery as the British bombed Fort McHenry in Baltimore Harbor?
    A. James Monroe **B. Francis Scott Key**
    C. Meriwether Lewis D. Zebulon Pike

(continued)

Part Two: Test Your Skills (18 points)

DIRECTIONS: In this chapter you read about the Louisiana Purchase. President Thomas Jefferson spent $15 million to gain more than 800,000 square miles of land for the United States. You also learned about the Lewis and Clark expedition through the unexplored lands. Think about the history of the United States up to that time. Then make three predictions about what you think will happen to the lands that were part of the Louisiana Purchase.

THE LOUISIANA PURCHASE

Louisiana Purchase

PREDICTIONS ABOUT THE LANDS OF THE LOUISIANA PURCHASE	
15. Prediction 1	Possible responses: Settlers will begin moving into the Louisiana Purchase territory or to the Pacific coast, and more states will soon be added to the United States. Valuable resources or fertile farmlands will be found in the Louisiana Purchase territory or on the Pacific coast, and
16. Prediction 2	people will need to travel throughout the new territory. A road or trail will be built across the Louisiana Purchase territory to take people to the Pacific coast. A transcontinental railroad will be built to link the Atlantic coast with the Pacific coast.
17. Prediction 3	

(continued)

Part Three: Apply What You Have Learned

DIRECTIONS: Complete each of the following activities.

18. **National Heroes (16 points)**
    Many people helped develop the United States in the early 1800s. Four of them are listed below. Because of their actions, these people are known as national heroes. In the space provided, briefly explain what each person did to become a national hero. **Possible responses:**

HERO	WHAT THE PERSON DID
Daniel Boone	He proved it was possible to travel west through the Cumberland Gap into Kentucky. He supervised the construction of the Wilderness Road, led settlers into Kentucky, and built the first settlement in Kentucky at Boonesborough.
Andrew Jackson	He defended the city of New Orleans from British attack during the War of 1812.
Francis Scott Key	He wrote a poem when he saw that the American flag was still flying after an all-night bombing of Fort McHenry during the War of 1812. His poem became our national anthem.
Zebulon Pike	He led an expedition into the southwestern part of the Louisiana Purchase territory. He went to Santa Fe in Spanish New Mexico. His actions led to the development of the Santa Fe Trail and the settlement of the Southwest.

19. **Essay (10 points)**
    One result of the War of 1812 was the growth of nationalism in the United States. Write one paragraph explaining what nationalism is and how it is shown by Americans today.
    Possible response:
    Nationalism is a patriotic feeling for one's own country. Displaying the American flag, celebrating national holidays, honoring military heroes, and singing the national anthem are all examples of how Americans show their feelings of nationalism today.

(continued)

ANSWERS

Chapter Test 12

Part One: Test Your Understanding (4 points each)

DIRECTIONS: *Use a name from the box below to complete each of the sentences that follow.*

> Frederick Douglass   Robert Fulton
> Francis Cabot Lowell   Horace Mann
> Samuel Slater   Harriet Beecher Stowe

1. A British factory worker named **Samuel Slater** brought the plans for a spinning machine to the United States.

2. **Francis Cabot Lowell** built a textile mill in which spinning, dyeing, and weaving all took place in the same factory.

3. **Robert Fulton** built a steamboat that he called the *Clermont*.

4. **Horace Mann** believed schools should be supported by taxes and should be free and open to all children.

5. **Harriet Beecher Stowe** wrote *Uncle Tom's Cabin*, which turned many people against slavery.

6. A runaway slave named **Frederick Douglass** told many people about his escape from slavery.

DIRECTIONS: *Circle the letter of the best answer.*

7. One thing that helped Andrew Jackson become President in 1828 was the fact that
   A. only people who could read and write were allowed to vote.
   B. married women could vote if they promised to vote the same way as their husbands.
   C. white men no longer had to own property to vote.
   D. free Africans were allowed to vote for the first time.

(continued)

---

8. Who was responsible for forcing the Cherokees off their land and onto the Trail of Tears?
   A. John Calhoun   B. James Monroe
   C. John Marshall   D. Andrew Jackson

9. Which of the following statements best describes the idea of Manifest Destiny?
   A. All American citizens should have the right to vote.
   B. All American women should have the right to own property.
   C. The United States should stretch from the Atlantic Ocean to the Pacific Ocean.
   D. All Native Americans should live in the land west of the Mississippi River.

10. In order to practice their religion where no one would bother them, the Mormons settled in what is now
    A. Texas.   B. Utah.
    C. Oregon.   D. Kansas.

11. The United States purchased California and much more land in the West after it won a war with
    A. Spain.   B. France.
    C. Britain.   D. Mexico.

12. Forty-niners were people who
    A. wanted to end slavery.
    B. traveled on the Oregon Trail.
    C. went to California to search for gold.
    D. supported the idea of states' rights.

13. Abolitionists worked to
    A. put an end to slavery.
    B. persuade people to use tax money to support schools.
    C. start a war with Mexico.
    D. give women the vote.

14. Which of these people was a former slave who traveled across the United States speaking out against slavery?
    A. Sojourner Truth   B. William Lloyd Garrison
    C. Harriet Beecher Stowe   D. Horace Mann

(continued)

Part Two: Test Your Skills (20 points)

DIRECTIONS: *Use the information in the double-bar graph to answer the questions.*

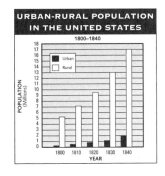

URBAN-RURAL POPULATION IN THE UNITED STATES
1800–1840

15. Between 1800 and 1840, did more people live in urban areas, such as New York City, or in rural areas? **in rural areas**

16. About how many people lived in rural areas in 1810? **about 7 million people**

17. In which year on the graph did the population in urban areas first pass one million? **in 1830**

18. To the closest million, what was the **total** (urban and rural) population of the United States in 1840? **19 million people**

19. The population in both areas grew a lot in the 40 years shown on the graph, but which population grew at the faster rate? **the urban population**

(continued)

Part Three: Apply What You Have Learned

DIRECTIONS: *Complete each of the following activities.*

20. **The Industrial Revolution (8 points)**
    The Industrial Revolution brought many changes to the United States. In the boxes below, list two changes in transportation and two changes in manufacturing brought about by the Industrial Revolution.

CHANGES IN TRANSPORTATION	CHANGES IN MANUFACTURING
Possible responses: new roadways, such as the National Road; the steamboat; the locomotive	Possible responses: mass production; interchangeable parts; Lowell's factory system

21. **Abolitionists Spread Their Message (6 points)**
    Abolitionists used speakers, newspapers, and books to tell Americans about slavery. In the chart below, give one example of each method.

METHODS	EXAMPLES
Speakers	Possible responses: Frederick Douglass or Sojourner Truth
Newspapers	*Freedom's Journal* or *The Liberator*
Books	*Uncle Tom's Cabin*

22. **Essay (10 points)**
    President Andrew Jackson and Vice President John C. Calhoun disagreed on the issues of sectionalism and states' rights. Write one paragraph explaining how the two leaders differed in their views.
    Possible response: The views of the President and the Vice President on sectionalism and states' rights were very different. President Jackson supported national unity and was opposed to sectionalism. Vice President Calhoun, on the other hand, believed strongly in sectionalism and the idea that states have final authority over the national government.

ANSWERS

Unit 6 Test

Part One: Test Your Understanding (4 points each)

DIRECTIONS: Circle the letter of the best answer.

1. Who led American settlers across the Appalachian Mountains into Kentucky?
   - A. Meriwether Lewis
   - B. Zebulon Pike
   - C. William Clark
   - **(D.)** Daniel Boone

2. Which of the following doubled the size of the United States?
   - A. the Monroe Doctrine
   - **(B.)** the Louisiana Purchase
   - C. the War of 1812
   - D. the Erie Canal

3. Which of the following people was responsible for American traders' carrying out an economic invasion of New Mexico?
   - **(A.)** Zebulon Pike
   - B. Stephen F. Austin
   - C. Brigham Young
   - D. Sam Houston

4. As a result of the War of 1812,
   - A. France established new colonies in North America.
   - **(B.)** a wave of nationalism swept the United States.
   - C. Spain was added to the United States.
   - D. the Americans defeated the British at the Battle of Washington, D.C.

5. The term *mass production* refers to
   - A. hiring many people to work in factories.
   - B. transporting goods, products, and people by water.
   - C. making parts by hand.
   - **(D.)** producing large amounts of goods at one time.

6. When the Erie Canal was finished, traders could transport goods by water from New York City to
   - **(A.)** the Great Lakes.
   - B. the Hudson River.
   - C. the Mississippi River.
   - D. the Ohio River valley.

7. Horace Mann was a leader in the movement for
   - A. women's rights.
   - **(C.)** public schools.
   - B. manifest destiny.
   - D. mass production.

(continued)

DIRECTIONS: *Match the description on the left with the correct name on the right. Write the correct letter in the space provided.*

8. **C** the name for the pass through the Appalachian Mountains into Kentucky

9. **E** the person who brought the plans for a spinning machine to the United States

10. **G** the Shoshone woman who acted as a translator for the Lewis and Clark expedition

11. **F** the abolitionist speaker who was a runaway slave

12. **A** the person who invented the first steam-powered boat

13. **D** the person who established a colony of Americans in Texas

14. **B** the American President who ignored the Supreme Court's ruling about the protection of the Cherokees

- A. Robert Fulton
- B. Andrew Jackson
- C. Cumberland Gap
- D. Stephen F. Austin
- E. Samuel Slater
- F. Frederick Douglass
- G. Sacagawea

(continued)

Part Two: Test Your Skills (20 points)

DIRECTIONS: *Use the information in the maps below to answer the questions.*

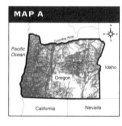
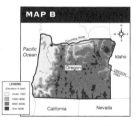

15. What physical feature did the people using the Oregon Trail want to avoid?

    They wanted to stay away from mountains.

16. Across what type of land did the people using the Oregon Trail hope to travel?

    They wanted to travel across flat land.

17. What is the highest elevation crossed by the Oregon Trail in Oregon? What is the lowest elevation? **The highest elevation is between 3,000 and 6,000 feet. The lowest elevation is less than 1,500 feet.**

18. Why did the Oregon Trail not go straight across Oregon to the Pacific Ocean?

    There are two mountain ranges people would have to go over if the trail went directly across Oregon.

(continued)

Part Three: Apply What You Have Learned

DIRECTIONS: *Complete each of the following activities.*

19. **Label the Map (14 points)**

    Use the map below to locate each of the items that follow. Show the location of each item by writing its letter on the map.

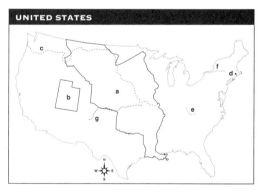

a. the area purchased from France by Thomas Jefferson in 1803

b. the place where Brigham Young and the Mormons settled

c. the path taken by Lewis and Clark

d. the location of Samuel Slater's textile mill

e. the Wilderness Road

f. the Erie Canal

g. the Santa Fe Trail

(continued)

ANSWERS

21. *Essay (10 points)*

In the early 1800s, there were several conflicts between the United States and Britain that led to the War of 1812. Write a paragraph describing one of those conflicts.

Possible response: One conflict between the United States and Britain concerned the Indian attacks that occurred after the Battle of Tippecanoe. Many people blamed the attacks on Britain, claiming that the British were giving guns to the Indians and talking against American settlers. Another conflict concerned the British practice of impressment. The British took American sailors off their ships and put them to work on British ships to stop Americans from trading with the French and other Europeans. The British practice of stopping American ships angered many Americans, who called on the U.S. government to declare war on Britain.

Individual Performance Task
Life on the Road

During the nineteenth century many people moved west from where they were living in the United States to start all over in a new place with new opportunities. In this activity you will create a diary for a person who moved west with his or her family.

Step 1 Select one of the following events as the basis for your diary:
- traveling with Daniel Boone to Kentucky
- traveling with Marcus and Narcissa Whitman to the Oregon Country
- traveling with Brigham Young to Utah

Step 2 Use a blank outline map of the United States to draw the route taken by the group you have chosen.

Step 3 Use your textbook and library resources to research the actions of your group.

Step 4 Write at least five diary entries for different events on different days and locations of the journey. Mention who is with you, the geography of the area you are passing through (landforms, vegetation, climate, and wildlife), and some of the events and activities of your daily life. You should be as creative as you can but remain historically accurate.

Step 5 Make a cover for your diary, and share the diary with your classmates.

Group Performance Task
Traveling West

A mobile is a piece of sculpture that hangs balanced in midair. Air currents cause the mobile to move. In this task your group will make a mobile that shows the paths taken by certain groups of settlers as they moved west.

Step 1 You will work in a group of at least five students.

Step 2 Your group should select one of the following:
- Daniel Boone and settlers going through the Cumberland Gap into Kentucky
- Brigham Young and the Mormons going to Utah
- the forty-niners heading for the California gold mines
- travelers along the Erie Canal
- Lewis and Clark exploring the lands of the Louisiana Purchase
- Marcus and Narcissa Whitman going to the Oregon Country
- travelers along the National Road
- Stephen F. Austin going to Texas to set up a colony

Step 3 Make a map showing the route of the group of settlers chosen. Draw a picture that shows some event or location connected with that group. Each member of your group should show a different scene.

Step 4 Paste your map and picture on both sides of a single sheet of construction paper.

Step 5 Use a coat hanger and string to create a mobile. Properly balance each person's artwork so that the mobile will move when it is hit by an air current. Hang the mobiles where others in the school can see them.

ANSWERS

Chapter Test 13

Part One: Test Your Understanding (4 points each)

DIRECTIONS: Circle the letter of the best answer.

1. The biggest farms in the South were located
   A. near salt marshes.
   B. along the Coastal Plain.
   C. far from the Mississippi River.
   D. near many factories.

2. Most of the people who lived in the South lived
   A. on small farms.
   B. in the cities.
   C. on plantations.
   D. along the sea coast.

3. In the early 1800s, life in the North changed more than life in the South because
   A. slavery became more important.
   B. the number of factories and cities increased.
   C. plantations became more popular.
   D. farmers raised more crops.

4. The invention of the cotton gin by Eli Whitney
   A. caused most of the textile mills in the North to close down.
   B. increased the need for slaves.
   C. decreased the need for cotton.
   D. made people move away from plantations.

5. The most serious disagreement between the North and the South concerned
   A. how much money farmers in the South should be paid for their crops.
   B. whether slavery should be allowed to spread to the frontier.
   C. how best to deal with the Indian peoples living in the North.
   D. whether to pay Eli Whitney for the invention of the cotton gin.

6. Slaves helped each other deal with their daily hardships by
   A. electing leaders to represent them.
   B. demanding that plantation owners pay them more money.
   C. keeping their traditions alive.
   D. writing letters of protest to the President.

(continued)

7. Who helped runaway slaves escape on the Underground Railroad?
   A. Dred Scott
   B. Nat Turner
   C. Jefferson Davis
   D. Harriet Tubman

8. Who persuaded Congress to agree to the Missouri Compromise?
   A. Henry Clay
   B. Abraham Lincoln
   C. Stephen Douglas
   D. Frederick Douglass

9. The Compromise of 1850
   A. encouraged western states to allow slavery.
   B. kept the number of free and slave states equal.
   C. required people to return runaway slaves to the South.
   D. limited the production of cotton.

10. The Kansas-Nebraska Act
    A. outlawed slavery in both Kansas and Nebraska.
    B. led to fighting in Kansas between people for and against slavery.
    C. gave the vote to slaves living in these two places.
    D. offered public education to slaves living in Kansas and Nebraska.

11. In the case of Dred Scott, the Supreme Court ruled that
    A. Scott was property and should not be given his freedom.
    B. slavery should be outlawed in the United States.
    C. slaves should have the same rights as other American citizens.
    D. Congress had the right to outlaw slavery in the Wisconsin Territory.

12. Abraham Lincoln joined the Republican party in order to
    A. make sure each state could decide the slavery question for itself.
    B. run for the U.S. House of Representatives.
    C. fight against the spread of slavery.
    D. work with Stephen Douglas.

13. Shortly after Lincoln was elected President in 1860, a group of Southern states
    A. withdrew from the Union and formed their own country.
    B. agreed to abolish slavery in the next five years.
    C. made plans to stop the spread of slavery to the new states.
    D. passed laws to protect the rights of slaves.

14. The president of the Confederacy was
    A. Jefferson Davis.
    B. James Forten.
    C. Roger B. Taney.
    D. Eli Whitney.

(continued)

Part Two: Test Your Skills (16 points)

DIRECTIONS: Use the graph below to answer the questions that follow.

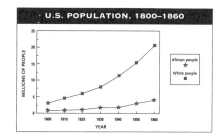

U.S. POPULATION, 1800–1860

15. Approximately how many African people were living in the United States in 1860?
    almost 3 million African people

16. In which decade did the population of white people increase the most?
    the 1850s

17. Based on this graph, what was the **total** population of white people and African people in the United States in 1860?
    about 25 million people

18. What conclusions can you draw from this graph?
    Possible responses: There were more than six times as many white people as African people in the United States in 1860; the population of white people in the United States grew much faster than the population of African people during the 1800s.

(continued)

Part Three: Apply What You Have Learned

DIRECTIONS: Complete each of the following activities.

19. **The Slave Codes (6 points)**
    Most states in the South in 1860 had slave codes, laws that shaped the day-to-day lives of enslaved people. List three ways that the lives of slaves were shaped by these slave codes.

    Possible responses: Slaves were not allowed to leave their owner's land. Slaves were not allowed to meet in groups. Slaves were not allowed to buy goods. Slaves were not allowed to sell goods. Slaves were not allowed to learn to read and write.

20. **What Do They Have in Common? (12 points)**
    Listed below are famous people who lived during the 1800s. Form four pairs of people and explain why you grouped them.

    | General Beauregard | John Brown | Henry Clay |
    | Jefferson Davis | Stephen Douglas | Abraham Lincoln |
    | Harriet Tubman | Nat Turner | Eli Whitney |

    Possible responses.

Pairs of People	Reason for Placing Them Together
Brown and Turner	Both took action to oppose slavery.
Lincoln and Douglas	Both ran for public office.
Davis and Beauregard	Both were Confederates.
Tubman and Lincoln	Both wanted slavery to end.

21. **Essay (10 points)**
    Stephen Douglas and Abraham Lincoln had very different ideas about how the question of slavery should be settled. Write a paragraph explaining how the two men differed in their viewpoints concerning slavery.
    Possible response: Stephen Douglas thought that each new state should decide the slavery question for itself. He believed that was what the country's founders had intended and what the Kansas-Nebraska Act allowed. Abraham Lincoln, on the other hand, believed that the framers of the Constitution intended and expected slavery to end. He argued that slavery should not be allowed to spread to the West.

ANSWERS

Chapter Test 14

Part One: Test Your Understanding (4 points each)

DIRECTIONS: *Circle the letter of the best answer.*

1. What new state was formed out of a slave state by people who were against slavery and wanted to remain in the Union?
   - A. Alabama
   - B. Kansas
   - C. Nebraska
   - (D.) West Virginia

2. An early Northern plan for fighting the war was based on
   - A. invading the border states.
   - B. having Indian allies capture the Confederate capital.
   - (C.) cutting off Southern trade by setting up a blockade.
   - D. invading Georgia and Alabama by sea.

3. The Confederate states
   - A. hoped to keep the war only in the South.
   - (B.) hoped that Britain and France would help them fight the war.
   - C. had more people, factories, and railroads than the Northern states.
   - D. welcomed all women who wanted to become soldiers.

4. Which of the following happened when President Abraham Lincoln signed the Emancipation Proclamation?
   - A. Great Britain and France were allowed to buy Southern cotton.
   - B. Most of the border states switched sides and joined the Confederacy.
   - (C.) The Union fought against both the Confederacy and slavery.
   - D. All of the slaves in the United States were freed.

5. General Grant's victory in the siege of Vicksburg was important because
   - A. it was the first battle won by the Union army.
   - B. it strengthened the Confederate army.
   - (C.) it gave the Union control of the Mississippi River.
   - D. it caused the South to surrender and end the Civil War.

6. In the Gettysburg Address, President Abraham Lincoln
   - A. issued the Emancipation Proclamation and freed the slaves.
   - (B.) honored the soldiers who had died fighting for liberty and equality.
   - C. named General Ulysses S. Grant to lead the Union army.
   - D. created the Freedmen's Bureau to help Africans in the South.

(continued)

7. "The soldiers did not have enough food. Many of them were nearly starving. Their clothes were dirty and torn." This statement best describes
   - (A.) Confederate troops just before General Lee surrendered.
   - B. Union troops at the end of the siege of Vicksburg.
   - C. Confederate troops after they captured Savannah, Georgia.
   - D. Union troops at the Battle of Gettysburg.

8. Which of these events happened **last**?
   - (A.) President Lincoln was assassinated.
   - B. General Lee surrendered to General Grant at Appomattox.
   - C. The Civil War ended.
   - D. General Sherman destroyed the city of Atlanta.

9. Slavery in the United States was ended forever by the passage of the
   - A. First Amendment.
   - B. Fourteenth Amendment.
   - C. Freedmen's Bureau.
   - (D.) Thirteenth Amendment.

10. The most important work of the Freedmen's Bureau was
    - A. helping former slaves find their family members.
    - B. helping former slaves find jobs in Northern factories.
    - (C.) educating the newly freed slaves.
    - D. making loans to the newly freed slaves so that they could buy plantations.

11. The black codes were laws that
    - (A.) limited the freedom of African Americans.
    - B. gave African Americans their own land to farm.
    - C. made African Americans citizens of the United States.
    - D. allowed African Americans to travel freely throughout the United States.

DIRECTIONS: *Match the person on the left with the description on the right. Write the correct letter in the space provided.*

12. **C** Clara Barton	A. led Union soldiers through Georgia on the March to the Sea	
13. **A** William T. Sherman	B. became President after the assassination of Abraham Lincoln	
14. **B** Andrew Johnson	C. helped sick and wounded Union soldiers during the Civil War	

(continued)

Part Two: Test Your Skills (24 points)

DIRECTIONS: *You learned about the problems and the difficult decisions Abraham Lincoln and Jefferson Davis had to make as supplies ran out at Fort Sumter. The first chart shows how Lincoln might have made his decision. Imagine you are Jefferson Davis. Use what you have learned about making decisions and about Fort Sumter to complete the second chart.*

PROBLEM: FORT SUMTER MIGHT SURRENDER TO THE SOUTH.

Possible Solutions:	Consequence of Each Solution:
Send supplies to the fort.	Southerners might attack the fort.
Send troops to the fort.	Southerners would surely attack the fort.
Do nothing at all.	After a while, the fort would surrender to the South.

Decision: Send supplies and wait to see what happens.

PROBLEM: LINCOLN HAS ANNOUNCED THAT HE WILL SEND SUPPLY SHIPS TO FORT SUMTER.

Possible Solutions:	Consequence of Each Solution:
15. Attack the fort **after** the supply ships arrive.	Possible response: The fort might repel the attack.
16. Attack the fort **before** the supply ships arrive.	Possible response: The South will win the fort, but the result could be war.
17. Do nothing at all.	Possible response: The fort will remain under Union control.

18. **Decision:** Possible response: Attack the fort before the supply ships arrive.

(continued)

Part Three: Apply What You Have Learned

DIRECTIONS: *Complete each of the following activities.*

19. **Famous People (10 points)**
    Listed below are the names of famous people who played a role in the Civil War and Reconstruction. Form two groups of names that go together. A group must have at least two names in it. You may use a name in more than one group. After you form a group, write a brief explanation of why you formed that group. An example has been done for you.

Clara Barton	Ulysses S. Grant	Andrew Johnson
Robert E. Lee	Abraham Lincoln	William H. Seward
William T. Sherman	Sally Tomkins	Harriet Tubman

Example: Lee, Grant — Civil War generals

Possible responses:

Barton, Tomkins—both army nurses

Lincoln, Johnson—both United States Presidents

20. **Essay (10 points)**
    Imagine that you are Robert E. Lee. Last night, April 18, 1861, President Lincoln asked you to take command of the Union army. Shortly after that, you learned that your home state of Virginia had seceded from the Union. You thought long and hard about whether you should accept Lincoln's offer. Write an entry for April 19, 1861, in your journal about your decision.
    Possible response:
    Last night President Lincoln asked me to head the Union army. This would be a great honor. But last night I also heard that my beloved Virginia has decided to secede from the Union. I am sure that Confederate leaders will also be asking me to serve in its army and to fight for Virginia. It is a difficult decision that I have to make. But I cannot fight against my friends and neighbors. I must turn down President Lincoln's request.

CHAPTER 14 TEST   Assessment Program 115
116   Assessment Program   CHAPTER 14 TEST
CHAPTER 14 TEST   Assessment Program 117
118   Assessment Program   CHAPTER 14 TEST

ANSWER KEY   Assessment Program 201

ANSWERS

Unit 7 Test

Part One: Test Your Understanding (4 points each)

DIRECTIONS: Circle the letter of the best answer.

1. Why was slavery important in the Southern states?
   - **A.** Slaves were needed to produce cotton and other crops.
   - B. Southern factories depended on slave labor.
   - C. Slaves were the only people who could read and write.
   - D. Slaves were needed to build the railroads.

2. Both Nat Turner and John Brown
   - A. helped Henry Clay with the Missouri Compromise.
   - **B.** led slave rebellions.
   - C. helped runaway slaves get to Northern cities.
   - D. were free Africans living in New Orleans.

3. People living in the slave communities helped each other cope with hardships by
   - A. making sure they were paid for their work.
   - B. electing leaders to represent them.
   - C. writing rules for all slaves to follow.
   - **D.** keeping their traditions alive.

4. The Underground Railroad was important because it
   - A. brought Northern products to the Southern states.
   - **B.** helped slaves escape from the South.
   - C. carried Southern cotton to the Northern textile mills.
   - D. was a low-cost way for all Southerners to travel.

5. Before the Civil War, most free Africans
   - A. lived on Southern plantations.
   - B. could vote and run for office.
   - **C.** faced difficulties in making a living.
   - D. moved to the western frontier states.

6. The Missouri Compromise
   - A. forced seven states to leave the Union.
   - B. made California a state.
   - C. stopped the activities on the Underground Railroad.
   - **D.** kept the number of free states and slave states equal.

(continued)

7. The Missouri Compromise and the Compromise of 1850
   - **A.** tried to settle the question of slavery in the western states.
   - B. limited the production of cotton.
   - C. were both written by Stephen Douglas.
   - D. allowed runaway slaves to live in the free states.

8. The Kansas-Nebraska Act led to
   - A. the decision to allow two more free states to join the Union.
   - B. the decision to allow Dred Scott to become a United States citizen.
   - C. passage of the Compromise of 1850.
   - **D.** violence between people who supported slavery and those who opposed it.

9. Which of the following statements best describes Abraham Lincoln's view on slavery before he became President?
   - A. He wanted to end slavery in the South.
   - B. He believed the framers of the Constitution wanted slavery to continue.
   - **C.** He was against the spread of slavery to new states.
   - D. He wanted to send runaway slaves back to Southern states.

10. Why was the battle at Fort Sumter important?
    - A. It showed how strong the Union army was.
    - B. It demonstrated the importance of sea power.
    - C. It was caused by the assassination of President Lincoln.
    - **D.** It marked the start of the Civil War.

11. Those states that remained in the Union after the Civil War started and that still allowed slavery were called
    - A. slave states.
    - B. rebel states.
    - C. Confederate states.
    - **D.** border states.

12. The First Battle of Bull Run was important because it demonstrated that the South
    - A. had very poor military leaders.
    - B. could only win battles fought on its own territory.
    - **C.** was more powerful than the North had expected.
    - D. had difficulty getting enough soldiers for its army.

13. Which of the following statements about African American soldiers in the Civil War is correct?
    - A. Fewer than 1,000 Africans served in the Union army.
    - **B.** Africans bravely served and died in many battles.
    - C. Many Africans served in the Confederate army.
    - D. The Emancipation Proclamation prevented Africans from serving in the army.

(continued)

14. The Confederacy was cut into two parts after the Union victory at the Battle of
    - A. Gettysburg.
    - B. Manassas Junction.
    - **C.** Vicksburg.
    - D. Savannah.

15. After the Civil War, the Freedmen's Bureau was established to
    - A. return plantations to their former owners.
    - B. give African Americans the right to vote.
    - C. encourage African Americans to move North.
    - **D.** build schools and educate former slaves.

16. Many members of Congress wanted to change President Johnson's plan for Reconstruction because
    - A. they wanted to be more fair to the Southern states than Johnson had been.
    - B. they agreed with the black codes.
    - C. Johnson had been impeached.
    - **D.** former slaves in some Southern states were being treated harshly.

(continued)

Part Two: Test Your Skills (20 points)

DIRECTIONS: Use the maps below to answer the questions that follow.

Map 1

Map 2

17. What is the distance between Memphis and Vicksburg on Map 1?

    about 200 miles

18. What is the distance between Vicksburg and Jackson on Map 1?

    about 50 miles _____ on Map 2? **about 50 miles**

19. Which cities on Map 2 did the Union army probably pass through during the siege of Vicksburg?

    Jackson, Greenville

20. Which map would you use if you wanted to visit Vicksburg? Explain.

    Possible response: Map 2, because it shows the area in more detail

(continued)

ANSWERS

Part Three: Apply What You Have Learned

DIRECTIONS: Complete each of the following activities.

21. *Protesting Slavery (6 points)*
Describe three methods used by enslaved people to protest slavery.
Possible responses:

a. They secretly damaged the plantation by breaking tools, leaving gates

open, letting boats drift away, and hiding household goods.

b. They acted as if they did not understand what they had been told and

said that they would try to do better.

c. They participated in rebellions.

22. *Essay (10 points)*
Imagine that you are the son or daughter of a conductor on the
Underground Railroad. Write a letter to your closest friend, describing
your family's experiences while taking part in the work of the
Underground Railroad.
Accept all reasonable responses.

Individual Performance Task
Gettysburg Time Capsule

A *time capsule* is a sealed container that holds articles and/or written documents that are representative of a specific time period and place. A time capsule is buried and preserved by people in one time period for people in a future age.

On November 19, 1863, President Abraham Lincoln went to Gettysburg, Pennsylvania, to dedicate the national cemetery for the soldiers who had died during the Battle of Gettysburg. A special memorial was built to honor the individuals who had fought so bravely in the battle. A time capsule was buried near that memorial. Your task is to imagine that you are in charge of the time capsule. As the person in charge, you must do two things:
- Select six items that will go into the time capsule.
- Explain why you have chosen each item.

These items should be representative of the time period of the Civil War. They should be items that would help someone in today's world better understand the events of the Civil War and the men and women who were alive at that time. Your teacher will tell you what resources you may use to decide what you would put into the time capsule.

Time-Capsule Items	Reasons for Including Them
_____	_____
_____	_____
_____	_____
_____	_____
_____	_____
_____	_____

Group Performance Task
You Are There

Radio stations often have news and current-events programs in which a reporter speaks with two or three different people to get their reactions and opinions about a specific individual or event. In this task the class will be divided into groups of four or five students. Each group will create a script of a radio news interview that might have taken place at the end of the Civil War.

One member of each group will act as the radio news reporter, and the other members will act as different people who were living at the end of the Civil War. Together, group members will create a set of written questions for the reporter to ask and a set of written answers to the questions. Then you will present your material to the class as if it were a live radio broadcast. Be sure that your script is representative of the people and the time period immediately following the war.

The people who might be included in your group are:
- a former slave
- a Northern soldier
- an African who served in the Union army
- a Southern soldier
- Clara Barton
- President Andrew Johnson
- General Ulysses S. Grant
- General Robert E. Lee
- Harriet Tubman

The questions that the radio reporter might ask are:
- What are your feelings and emotions at the end of the war?
- What political events during the war were important to you?
- What financial problems do you have today?
- What happened to your family during the war?
- How has the war changed your community?
- What do you think the future will bring for the country?

ANSWERS

Chapter Test 15

Part One: Test Your Understanding (4 points each)

DIRECTIONS: *Match the description on the left with the correct word or name on the right. Write the correct letter in the space provided.*

1. **A** economic system in which people are able to start and run their own businesses

2. **I** money needed to run a business

3. **D** business that sells shares of stock to investors

4. **M** person who takes a chance by opening up a business

5. **C** what made many inland cities important centers of industry

6. **L** what workers did to get factory owners to listen to them

7. **O** group of workers who take action to improve their working conditions

8. **H** organization made up of many groups

9. **F** a city neighborhood of Spanish-speaking people

10. **J** what many people born in America feared they would lose to immigrants

11. **B** entry place into the United States for most immigrants from Europe

A. free enterprise

B. Ellis Island

C. railroad

D. corporation

E. skyscrapers

F. barrio

G. trolley car

H. federation

I. capital resources

J. jobs

K. naturalization

L. strike

M. entrepreneur

N. settlement houses

O. labor union

12. **K** way for immigrants to become United States citizens

13. **N** community centers in cities that helped immigrants learn skills

14. **E** steel-framed buildings that helped cities grow upward

15. **G** invention that helped make it possible for more people to move to suburbs

(continued)

Part Two: Test Your Skills (24 points)

DIRECTIONS: *Use the time zone map below to answer the questions that follow.*

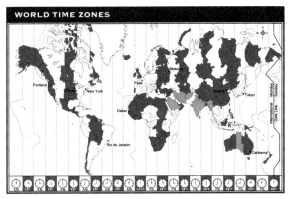

WORLD TIME ZONES

16. When it is 4:00 P.M. in Rio de Janeiro, what time is it in Chicago? **1:00 P.M.**

17. When it is 7:00 A.M. in New York, what time is it in Moscow? **2:00 P.M.**

18. When it is 10:00 A.M. in Tokyo, what time is it in Paris? **1:00 A.M.**

19. When it is 7:00 A.M. in Portland, what time is it in Beijing? **11:00 P.M.**

(continued)

Part Three: Apply What You Have Learned

DIRECTIONS: *Complete each of the following activities.*

20. *Becoming a Citizen (6 points)*
    Many immigrants felt that becoming United States citizens was very important. To become a citizen, an immigrant had to complete a series of steps. List these steps below.

    a. **Immigrants had to live in the United States for five years, pass a**

    b. **test on the government and history of the United States, and take an**

    c. **oath promising allegiance to the United States.**

21. *Essay (10 points)*
    At the end of the nineteenth century and the beginning of the twentieth century, factory workers and new immigrants living in American cities faced many problems. Choose one of these groups and explain in one paragraph the problems they faced living and working in the cities.
    Possible responses:
    Factory workers had to deal with low wages, unsafe working conditions, and many accidents. In addition, many adults were without jobs while children worked long hours under harsh conditions.

    New immigrants in the cities faced many problems. Among these problems were poor housing, disease, no garbage collection, many fires, and crime.

ANSWERS

Chapter Test 16

Chapter Test 16

Part One: Test Your Understanding (4 points each)

DIRECTIONS: *Circle the letter of the best answer.*

1. The purpose of the Homestead Act was to
   A. give companies money to build a railroad across the country.
   B. encourage people to settle on the Great Plains.
   C. open the first cattle trail to the railroads.
   D. end the battles between ranchers and farmers.

2. Railroad owners wanted more people to settle on the Great Plains because
   A. settlers would use the railroads for travel.
   B. they needed more people to build railroad tracks.
   C. they needed sharecroppers to farm the land owned by the railroads.
   D. settlers would grow cotton and ship it to the South.

3. Settlers on the Great Plains used sod to build their houses because
   A. sod houses were cleaner than other buildings.
   B. there were few trees that could be used for wood.
   C. houses made from wood were too cold in the winters on the Great Plains.
   D. the railroads paid people to live in sod houses.

4. The person who invented a stronger plow to help people cut through the thick sod was
   A. Joseph Glidden.   B. Richard King.
   C. James Oliver.   D. George Custer.

5. Which of the following caused some farmers to leave their farms on the Great Plains?
   A. railroads   **B.** bad weather
   C. immigrants   D. barbed wire

6. After Joseph McCoy opened his stockyards near some railroad tracks in Abilene, Kansas,
   A. many farmers moved to the Great Plains.
   B. the Indians started moving to the reservations.
   C. ranchers started moving herds of cattle to the "cow towns."
   D. the mining boom in the West ended.

(continued)

CHAPTER 16 TEST

Assessment Program **131**

---

7. What were long drives?
   A. transportation by railroad
   B. special areas of farmland on the Great Plains given to homesteaders
   C. the path of the buffalo migration on the Great Plains
   D. trips on which cowhands moved large numbers of cattle to the railroads

8. The range wars were caused by
   A. the use of barbed wire.   B. the British.
   C. the steel plow.   D. railroad owners.

9. What happened during a mining boom?
   A. Most people lost all of their money.
   B. People moved away from mining areas.
   C. Gold, silver, and copper mines were closed.
   D. There was quick economic growth.

10. Which of the following caused some mining towns to become ghost towns?
   A. The range wars destroyed all the buildings in the towns.
   B. The mines ran out of gold, silver, or copper.
   C. The railroads moved away.
   D. The vaqueros ordered everyone to leave the towns.

11. Law and order was maintained in the mining towns by
   A. the United States Army.   B. county sheriffs.
   C. Vigilance Committees.   D. the Union army.

12. The most important resource of the Plains Indians was
   A. the buffalo.   B. wheat.
   C. the horse.   D. corn.

13. Why did General George Custer take his soldiers to the Little Bighorn River in 1876?
   A. to open a new railroad through the Black Hills
   B. to protect cowhands on long drives across the Sioux reservation
   C. to help miners in a boom town
   D. to take back land the government had given to the Sioux

14. Why did U.S. Army soldiers chase the Nez Perces for more than 1,700 miles?
   A. because the Nez Perces were living on land that contained gold
   B. to punish them for defeating Custer and his soldiers
   C. because the Nez Perces were trying to escape to Canada
   D. to stop them from going to war with the Sioux

(continued)

132 Assessment Program

CHAPTER 16 TEST

Part Two: Test Your Skills (25 points)

DIRECTIONS: *Use the climographs to answer the questions that follow.*

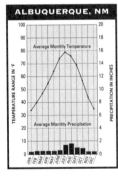

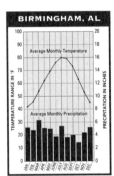

15. What is the wettest month in each city?
   Albuquerque, August; Birmingham, March

16. What is the average temperature in each city in April?
   Albuquerque, 55° F; Birmingham, 62° F

17. What is the coldest month in each city?
   Albuquerque and Birmingham, January

18. What is the warmest month in each city?
   Albuquerque and Birmingham, July

19. Which city receives more precipitation? **Birmingham**

(continued)

CHAPTER 16 TEST

Assessment Program **133**

Part Three: Apply What You Have Learned

DIRECTIONS: *Complete each of the following activities.*

20. *Indian Reservations (9 points)*
   Indian reservations were created by the United States government as places where the Native American peoples could live. Describe how each of the groups below resisted living on reservations.

   Sioux
   Possible response: The Sioux fought back at the Battle of Little Bighorn.

   Nez Perces
   Possible response: The Nez Perces tried to relocate to Canada.

   Apaches
   Possible response: The Apaches attacked Arizona settlers and hid from the U.S. Army for five years.

21. *Essay (10 points)*
   The western part of the United States was settled mainly by farmers and miners. Explain in one paragraph how farmers and miners were alike and how they were different.
   Possible response:
   Farmers and miners were alike in some ways. Both had to work hard and had to face the hardships of life in the West. Both usually had very little money. Farmers and miners also were different in some ways. Farmers usually lived and worked with their families, while miners usually lived near the mines and worked alone. Farmers stayed in one place, while miners often moved from place to place.

134 Assessment Program

CHAPTER 16 TEST

ANSWER KEY

Assessment Program **205**

ANSWERS

Unit 8 Test

Part One: Test Your Understanding (4 points each)

DIRECTIONS: *Circle the letter of the best answer.*

1. Which of the following was the first kind of business to set up corporations?
   A. bonanza farms (B.) railroads
   C. steel mills D. refining

2. With the growth of industries such as steel and oil, new industrial cities developed
   A. near good harbors. B. in the West.
   C. near the oceans. (D.) inland.

3. To try to improve their working conditions, workers in the late 1800s sometimes
   A. fought against the labor unions.
   B. volunteered to be fired so that family members would be hired.
   (C.) went on strike.
   D. offered to work longer hours for less pay.

4. What were the two basic goals of the American Federation of Labor?
   A. to end strikes and hire more children as workers
   B. to get a five-day workweek and summer vacations
   (C.) to get higher wages and a shorter workday
   D. to do away with accident insurance and hire fewer children as workers

5. Many Americans wanted to stop the immigration of Asians because
   (A.) they worried that Asian immigrants would take their jobs.
   B. they did not want the Asian immigrants to create any more barrios in the Southwest.
   C. the law required that Asian immigrants be paid more than other people.
   D. the eastern part of the United States was becoming too crowded.

6. During the early 1900s, many African American families moved to the northern cities because
   A. they wanted to get better land to farm.
   B. they were forced to leave the southern states.
   C. the climate in the North was better.
   (D.) there were more jobs in the northern cities.

(continued)

UNIT 8 TEST   Assessment Program 135

7. What was the purpose of a settlement house?
   A. to give cowhands a place to stay after the cattle drives
   (B.) to help immigrants learn American skills and customs
   C. to teach farmers about irrigation
   D. to improve the education of schoolteachers

8. Many settlers in the West bought land at low prices from the
   A. Indians. B. vaqueros.
   (C.) railroads. D. miners.

9. Most houses on the Great Plains were made with
   A. adobe. B. bricks.
   (C.) sod. D. logs.

10. It was important for ranchers to get their cattle to northern cities because
   A. people in the southern cities did not eat beef.
   B. all the cattle buyers in the country lived in the North.
   C. northern cities had more open range in which to raise cattle.
   (D.) they could earn a higher profit in the northern cities.

11. How did Joseph Glidden help to bring an end to the Cattle Kingdom?
   A. He made the first steel plow.
   B. He founded the first mining town.
   (C.) He invented barbed wire.
   D. He built the first transcontinental railroad.

12. When did mining towns experience the most rapid population growth?
   A. when windmills were invented
   B. when people moved away from the mines
   C. when the gold, silver, and copper mines closed
   (D.) when there was quick economic growth

13. The traditional way of life of the Plains Indians came to an end when
   A. the cattle drives began. B. the range wars ended.
   (C.) settlers killed off the buffalo. D. the mining boom started.

14. Geronimo and his people refused to stay on the reservation because
   A. they wanted to return to the Black Hills of South Dakota.
   (B.) there was not enough food on their reservation.
   C. there was no railroad on their reservation.
   D. they wanted to follow the buffalo on their migration.

(continued)

136 Assessment Program   UNIT 8 TEST

Part Two: Test Your Skills (24 points)

DIRECTIONS: *Problem solving is an important skill. Homesteaders on the Great Plains faced many problems as they made a new life in this region. One of the problems they had to solve was that of getting water to their families and their animals. For each possible solution to the problem listed in the table below, give reasons as to why it is a good solution or why it is a bad solution.*

SOLVING A PROBLEM	
Problem: Getting water to the farms on the Great Plains	
Possible Solution	Results of Solution
15. Build pipelines to carry water from rivers to the farms.	Possible response: Building pipelines from rivers to the farms would be very expensive. In many parts of the Great Plains, there are not enough rivers to supply all the farms.
16. Build dams on streams to store water for the farms.	Possible response: Building dams would be very expensive. If dams were built across streams, there would not be enough water for any farms downstream from the dams.
17. Bring in water by wagons or by railroads to the farms.	Possible response: Bringing in water by wagons or by railroads would not be practical. Wagons could not carry enough water and railroad tracks would have to be laid to every farm.
18. Build windmills to pump water from the ground for the farms.	Possible response: Windmills could be used on the Great Plains because it is windy there and because there is enough water underground for the needs of many farms.

(continued)

UNIT 8 TEST   Assessment Program 137

Part Three: Apply What You Have Learned

DIRECTIONS: *Complete each of the following activities.*

19. Magic Square (10 points)
From the statements below, select the best match for each name listed. Put the number of the name with the matching statement letter in the magic square. You can check your answers by adding across each row or down each column. You should get the same number each way. Record that number in the magic number space.

a = 2	b = 4	c = 9
d = 7	e = 3	f = 5
g = 6	h = 8	i = 1

Magic Number = 15

1. Sitting Bull
2. Samuel Gompers
3. George Westinghouse
4. William Jenney
5. Henry Bessemer
6. Chief Joseph
7. Joseph McCoy
8. Jane Addams
9. James Oliver

a. started the American Federation of Labor

b. built the first skyscraper

c. invented a steel plow that helped farmers on the Great Plains

d. built the stockyards at Abilene, Kansas, that started the cattle drives

e. invented the safety brake for trains

f. created a new, improved process for making steel

g. led the Nez Perces on an escape to Canada

h. started Hull House in Chicago to teach new skills to immigrants

i. led the Sioux at the Battle of Little Bighorn

(continued)

138 Assessment Program   UNIT 8 TEST

ANSWERS

20. Essay (10 points)

The government had different policies toward unions, immigrants, and Indians at the end of the nineteenth century. Choose one of these groups. Explain in one paragraph the government's policy toward that group.

Possible responses:

Unions—The government's policy toward unions was to support free enterprise and business. The government did not help the unions in their battles with factory owners.

Immigrants—The government passed laws to keep Chinese and Japanese immigrants out of the United States. The government also created naturalization, which allows immigrants to become citizens of the United States.

Indians—The government used force to take away land that belonged to the Indians. The government also used force to make Indians live on reservations.

Individual Performance Task
Have We Got a Deal for You!

Many businesses use a brochure to advertise to the public. In this task you are going to create a brochure that could have been used by one of the transcontinental railroads to get people to move into the areas along its path.

Step 1 Use library materials and your textbooks to find the paths of the first four transcontinental railroads (Northern Pacific, Union Pacific-Central Pacific, Santa Fe, and Southern Pacific). Select one of these railroads. Then select an area along the railroad that you will advertise in the brochure.

Step 2 Decide who will read the brochure. Will it be people immigrating to the United States? Will it be people who want to move from the East to the West? The information you give will depend on who your readers will be.

Step 3 Determine what information you will put in the brochure. You must include the name and address of the railroad company and a map of the area you are advertising. You should also tell in the brochure what is good about the area you are advertising. You might cover some of these topics and add others of your own.

- climate
- mineral resources
- religious freedom
- water resources
- crops
- political freedom
- lumber resources
- wild animals
- land prices
- soil
- plants

Step 4 Make a rough draft of the brochure. Put information on the front of the brochure that will make people want to open it and read further. Draw the map on the back of the brochure, along with the name and address of the railroad company. (You do not have to use a real address. Make up an address in the area you are advertising.) After you have made the rough draft, show it to a classmate and ask whether all the material is clear.

Step 5 Make a final copy. Present the brochure to the rest of the class.

Group Performance Task
Words of the Old West

A *lexicon* is a collection of words. In this task your small group will create a book called *A Lexicon of the Old West.*

Step 1 With your group, brainstorm words from *A* to *Z* that deal with the West as covered in this unit. The words should be about farmers, ranchers, cowhands, miners, and Indians during the last years of the nineteenth century. For example, an *A* word might be *Abilene* and a *B* word might be *Bonanza Farm*. The letter does not have to be the first letter of the word. For example, an *X* word could be *Sioux*. Try to come up with as many words for each letter as possible.

Step 2 Help your group choose one word for each letter of the alphabet. It should be one for which a picture could be drawn to show its meaning or importance.

Step 3 Divide the letters of the alphabet among the members of the group. Each person should be responsible for about the same number of letters. Each student will create a page for the lexicon for each of his or her words. There should be three parts to each page.

> **Part 1** At the top of the page will be the words *A is for Abilene, B is for Bonanza Farm*, and so on.
>
> **Part 2** In the center of the page will be a drawing that shows the meaning of the word. For example, under *A is for Abilene* could be a drawing of a railroad train, a stockyard, and cattle being loaded on the train.
>
> **Part 3** At the bottom of the page will be a two-sentence explanation of the importance of the word. For example, you could write "Joseph McCoy built the first stockyards in Abilene, Kansas, in 1867. This was the beginning of the Cattle Kingdom and cattle drives." Be sure your sentences fit with your drawing.

Step 4 One student from the group should make a cover sheet for the lexicon. Another student should make a Table of Contents. In the Table of Contents, there should be one line for each letter. It should state the name of the page, for example, *A is for Abilene*, the name of the student responsible for the page, and the page number. When the lexicon is finished, your group can display it for others to enjoy.

ANSWERS

Chapter Test 17

Part One: Test Your Understanding (4 points each)

DIRECTIONS: *Circle the letter of the best answer.*

1. Americans became interested in Alaska
   A. as a good place to grow cotton.
   B. after gold was discovered there.
   C. until they realized that it had few natural resources.
   D. because it was so close to Germany.

2. Which of these Americans gained control of the land and trade in Hawaii?
   A. missionaries and sugar planters
   B. tobacco planters and cotton planters
   C. sea captains and merchants
   D. owners of fishing and whaling ships

3. Which two areas gained by the United States in the Spanish-American War remain U.S. territories today?
   A. Guam and Cuba
   B. Puerto Rico and Guam
   C. Puerto Rico and the Philippines
   D. Cuba and the Philippines

4. President Theodore Roosevelt wanted the United States to use its power in the world because
   A. most countries around the world considered the United States to be weak.
   B. he wanted to fight in all the world's wars.
   C. he wanted to force other countries to buy only American-made goods.
   D. he believed that events in the rest of the world affected the United States.

5. Why did the United States want to build the Panama Canal?
   A. to move the navy out of the Caribbean Sea into the Pacific
   B. to fight in the Spanish-American War
   C. to link American territories in the Atlantic and Pacific
   D. to increase trade between Mexico and the United States

6. The main goals of the progressives were to
   A. improve government and make life better.
   B. end wars and make peace.
   C. stop immigration and foreign trade.
   D. help farmers learn new ways and grow new crops.

(continued)

7. Theodore Roosevelt called his program of progressive reforms the
   A. Square Deal.   **B.** Promise to People Policy.
   C. Government in Action Program.   D. United Way.

8. Governor Robert La Follette started a merit system in Wisconsin to
   A. reduce the number of hours in a workday from 16 to 14.
   B. make sure that children could be hired for any jobs they wanted.
   C. make sure that people who got government jobs were qualified for them.
   D. make sure that young people who graduated from high school could read and write.

9. The goal of the National Association for the Advancement of Colored People was to
   A. help unions win the right to strike.
   B. achieve full civil rights for African Americans.
   C. stop the railroads from charging high fares.
   D. stop immigrants from coming to the United States.

10. Why did the United States enter World War I?
    A. Russia asked for its help.
    B. France started killing American soldiers.
    C. The Turkish navy sank the battleship *Maine*.
    D. German submarines sank American ships.

11. The most feared of the new weapons used in World War I was
    A. barbed wire.   **B.** poison gas.
    C. the machine gun.   D. the handgun.

12. How did women contribute to the war effort in World War I?
    A. They helped men fight in the trenches in France.
    B. They were drafted into the army and navy.
    C. They flew airplanes in battles over France.
    D. They took over the jobs left by men going to war.

13. American women won the right to vote with the passage of the
    A. Thirteenth Amendment.   **B.** Nineteenth Amendment.
    C. Fourteenth Amendment.   D. Tenth Amendment.

14. The members of Congress voted **not** to join the League of Nations because
    A. they wanted the United States to stay out of other countries' problems.
    B. the League refused to elect an American to head the organization.
    C. the League wanted the United States to pay for the organization.
    D. they believed that wars were the only way to win new territories.

(continued)

Part Two: Test Your Skills (24 points)

DIRECTIONS: **On May 7, 1915, a German U-boat sank the British passenger ship *Lusitania*. Americans were outraged, accusing the Germans of "piracy on the high seas." Germans defended the action, saying that the *Lusitania* was traveling in a war zone and that the ship was carrying weapons to help the British war effort. Leaders on both sides used propaganda to try to gain support for their cause. Read the quotation below by Germany's Baron von Schwarzenstein, and then read the statements that follow. Circle T if the statement is true and F if the statement is false.**

> *In the case of the* Lusitania *the German Ambassador even further warned Americans through the great American newspapers against taking passage thereon. Does a pirate act thus? . . . Nobody regrets more sincerely than we Germans the hard necessity of sending to their deaths hundreds of men. Yet the sinking was a justifiable act of war. . . . The scene of war is no golf links, the ships of belligerent powers no pleasure places. . . . We have sympathy with the victims and their relatives, of course, but did we hear anything about sympathy . . . when England adopted her diabolical plan of starving a great nation?*

T F   **15.** Baron von Schwarzenstein claimed that the sinking of the *Lusitania* was an act of war.

T F   **16.** Both facts and opinions are presented in the baron's statement.

T **F**   **17.** The statement was meant to convince people that Germany should not have attacked a passenger ship even though it was in a war zone.

T **F**   **18.** The baron said that Germans had no sympathy for the victims or their relatives.

T F   **19.** The baron accused Britain of trying to starve the people of Germany.

T F   **20.** Baron von Schwarzenstein's statement is propaganda.

(continued)

Part Three: Apply What You Have Learned

DIRECTIONS: **Complete each of the following activities.**

21. **Participants in World War I (10 points)**
    Identify the two sides that fought each other in World War I. Then list the countries that first made up each alliance.

    a. **Allied** _____ Powers   f. **Central** _____ Powers
    b. **Russia** _____   g. **Germany** _____
    c. **France** _____   h. **Austria-Hungary** _____
    d. **Britain** _____   i. **the Ottoman Empire** _____
    e. **Italy** _____   j. **Bulgaria** _____

22. **Essay (10 points)**
    Write a one-paragraph essay explaining how the progressives used the power of the federal government to make life better for Americans. Be sure to include the law or the name of the government agency involved.

    Possible response:
    The progressives used the power of the federal government to make life better for Americans. For example, they used this power to set rates on the railroads (Interstate Commerce Commission), to monitor the quality of food and drugs (Pure Food and Drug Act, Meat Inspection Act), and to conserve the nation's resources (national park system).

ANSWERS

Chapter Test 18

Part One: Test Your Understanding (4 points each)

DIRECTIONS: Circle the letter of the best answer.

1. Henry Ford found that he could produce cars less expensively by
   A. using plastic instead of steel for some car parts.
   B. hiring only immigrants to work in his factory.
   C. using a moving assembly line.
   D. using designs made in Japan.

2. Jazz developed from the musical heritage of
   A. Native Americans.   B. rock and roll.
   C. German immigrants.   **D.** African Americans.

3. What was the Harlem Renaissance?
   A. a system whereby people could pay a little money each month for consumer goods
   B. a program for rebuilding large areas of New York City after a fire
   C. the migration of African Americans from the North to the South during the 1920s
   D. a time of interest and activity in the arts among African American writers, musicians, and artists

4. The stock market crash of 1929 occurred because
   A. there were too many people without full-time jobs.
   B. more people wanted to sell stock than wanted to buy stock.
   C. farmers could not produce enough food for the country.
   D. World War I caused the economy to crash.

5. After the stock market crashed, many banks had to close because
   A. bankers had used bank money to invest in Roosevelt's Alphabet Soup.
   B. large numbers of people took their saved money out of banks in order to live.
   C. the government needed the banks' money to run its many programs.
   D. the government ordered them to do so.

6. How did the New Deal affect the federal government?
   A. The federal government lost power to the state governments.
   B. The New Deal let the President take the country to war.
   C. The federal government got more authority and more workers.
   D. The New Deal stopped government control over the railroads.

(continued)

7. The Works Progress Administration hired workers to
   A. take the place of union members who were on strike.
   B. invest government money in the stock market.
   C. take over the banks that had been closed.
   D. build roads, airports, and public buildings.

8. The building of hydroelectric dams helped economic development by
   A. allowing the government to sell electricity at low rates.
   B. allowing farmers to sell water at high rates.
   C. giving investors the opportunity to buy shares of stock in the dams.
   D. giving farmers more land on which to grow crops.

9. As the ruler of Germany, Adolf Hitler
   A. attacked United States naval bases in Hawaii.
   B. put only Jewish people into positions of leadership.
   C. caused the German stock market to crash.
   D. rebuilt Germany's economy by preparing for another war.

10. World War II began in Europe when
    A. Italy took over Ethiopia.   B. Japan invaded Manchuria.
    C. Germany invaded Poland.   D. Germany attacked France.

11. The United States entered World War II the day after
    A. Britain declared war on Germany.
    B. Russia invaded Britain.
    C. the Japanese bombed Pearl Harbor.
    D. the Germans attacked New York City.

12. How did the United States government make sure there were enough supplies to send to soldiers overseas?
    A. by closing many grocery stores   **B.** by rationing
    C. by helping farmers   D. by raising prices

13. During World War II, the United States government set up relocation camps for
    A. Native Americans.   B. German Americans.
    C. African Americans.   **D.** Japanese Americans.

14. What was the Holocaust?
    A. the German invasion and bombing of Poland
    B. Hitler's mass murder of European Jews
    C. German plans in World War II to invade eastern Europe
    D. the destruction of German cities by firebombs

(continued)

Part Two: Test Your Skills (16 points)

DIRECTIONS: Use the information in the time lines to answer the following questions.

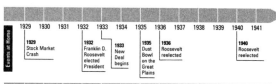

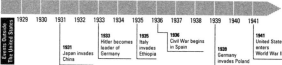

15. What was happening outside the United States at the same time as the Dust Bowl on the Great Plains?
    Italy was invading Ethiopia.

16. Did the United States enter World War II before or after the New Deal began?
    after the New Deal began

17. Was Franklin Roosevelt elected to office before or after Japan invaded China?
    after Japan invaded China

18. Which event took place first—the stock market crash or the invasion of Poland?
    the stock market crash

(continued)

Part Three: Apply What You Have Learned

DIRECTIONS: Complete each of the following activities.

19. **Economic Relationships (6 points)**
    Explain the relationships among consumer goods, advertisements, and installment buying by defining the terms in the chart below.

CONSUMER GOODS	ADVERTISEMENTS	INSTALLMENT BUYING
Possible responses: Consumer goods are products for personal use.	Advertisements encourage people to buy consumer goods.	Installment buying allows people to buy consumer goods over time.

20. **Which One Does Not Belong? (12 points)**
    In each of the groups of words below, there is one word or phrase that does not belong. Circle that word or phrase, and give a brief explanation as to why it does not belong with the others.
    Possible responses:
    a. front   island-hopping   **relocation camps**
    Front and *island-hopping* are words that apply to the fighting overseas in World War II. Relocation camps were set up in the United States during the war.

    b. **rationing**   free world   communism
    The free world and communist countries were on opposite sides in the Cold War. Rationing was the way the government controlled goods during World War II.

    c. Harlem Renaissance   jazz   **minimum wage**
    Harlem Renaissance and jazz both relate to African American tradition. Minimum wage applies to all workers.

21. **Essay (10 points)**
    Write a one-paragraph essay explaining why the Cold War developed.
    Possible response: After World War II, the United States and its allies, known as the free world, worked to stop the spread of communism. The Cold War developed out of hostilities between the free world and the communist nations. This "war" did not involve armies and shooting, but rather money and propaganda.

ANSWERS

Unit 9 Test

Part One: Test Your Understanding (4 points each)

DIRECTIONS: Circle the letter of the best answer.

1. Which of the following events led the United States into a war with Spain?
   A. the American attack on Manila
   B. the Spanish attack on Miami, Florida
   C. the sinking of the battleship *Maine*
   D. the firing on Fort Sumter

2. The Panama Canal is important to world trade because
   A. it links the Indian Ocean with the Caribbean Sea.
   B. it is the only body of water in the world large enough for cargo ships to travel on.
   C. it connects the Mississippi River to the Pacific Ocean.
   D. it provides a shortcut between the Atlantic and Pacific oceans.

3. President Theodore Roosevelt promoted the conservation of natural resources by
   A. making it illegal for hunters to shoot animals for sport.
   B. passing strong laws against pollution.
   C. forcing manufacturers to pay heavy fines for the use of raw materials.
   D. setting aside land for national parks and wilderness areas.

4. What was the purpose of Governor Robert La Follette's merit system?
   A. to give the government control over the meat industry
   B. to give government jobs only to people who were qualified
   C. to stop businesses from charging prices that were too high
   D. to stop strikes by workers' unions

5. What organization was formed in 1909 by W. E. B. Du Bois and other leaders to help African Americans?
   A. Interstate Commerce Commission
   B. Urban League
   C. Hull House
   D. National Association for the Advancement of Colored People

(continued)

UNIT 9 TEST

Assessment Program 151

---

6. During World War I, Russia, France, Italy, Britain, and the United States fought against the
   A. Allied Powers.
   B. Central Powers.
   C. Communist Powers.
   D. Axis Powers.

7. In World War I soldiers fought one another
   A. in tanks.
   B. in submarines.
   C. from ditches dug in the ground.
   D. with propaganda.

8. As a result of Charles Lindbergh's flight across the Atlantic Ocean,
   A. U.S. military leaders decided to use airplanes in World War I.
   B. people became more interested in air travel.
   C. the price of airplanes decreased.
   D. the Wright brothers decided to buy Lindbergh's airplane designs.

9. An important poet in the Harlem Renaissance was
   A. Carrie Chapman Catt.
   B. W. E. B. Du Bois.
   C. D. W. Griffith.
   D. Langston Hughes.

10. When the banks failed and Americans lost their money,
    A. people bought fewer goods and factory workers lost their jobs.
    B. people in France and Britain sent donations of food and money.
    C. only people who had invested in the stock market could pay for food.
    D. the government gave all homeless people free houses.

11. How did the New Deal affect the power and size of the federal government?
    A. The power and size of the federal government increased.
    B. The states gained more power than the federal government.
    C. Workers were able to take power away from the federal government by forming unions.
    D. The federal government became smaller but more powerful.

(continued)

152 Assessment Program

UNIT 9 TEST

---

12. After World War I, the countries of Germany, the Soviet Union, Spain, Italy, and Japan
    A. paid Britain and France for the costs of the war.
    B. were ruled by dictators.
    C. voted to become democratic countries.
    D. started the Cold War.

13. The United States entered World War II
    A. when Germany invaded Poland.
    B. when the United States started island-hopping.
    C. after Japan bombed Pearl Harbor.
    D. before the Philippines attacked Japan.

14. What caused Japan to surrender at the end of World War II?
    A. The Japanese army was trapped on Iwo Jima.
    B. Allied armies invaded the Japanese islands.
    C. The United States dropped two atomic bombs on Japan.
    D. Germany stopped giving the Japanese any aid.

(continued)

UNIT 9 TEST

Assessment Program 153

Part Two: Test Your Skills (24 points)

DIRECTIONS: Use the two maps below to answer the questions that follow.

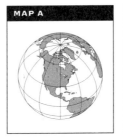

15. On which map are the meridians spaced equally? __on Map B__

16. On which map are the parallels spaced equally? __on Map A__

17. On which map do meridians get closer at the pole? __on Map A__

18. On which part of the maps do the land shapes appear the same?
    __in the center of the maps__

19. On which part of the maps are the land shapes the most different?
    __near the North Pole__

20. Which map shows direction more accurately?
    __Map B__

(continued)

154 Assessment Program

UNIT 9 TEST

ANSWER KEY

ANSWERS

Part Three: Apply What You Have Learned

DIRECTIONS: *Complete each of the following activities.*

21. Popular Entertainment (4 points)
List two new forms of entertainment that became popular in the 1920s.
Possible responses:

listening to the radio

going to the movies

22. Participants in World War II (6 points)
During World War II, the Axis Powers fought against the Allies. List the countries that made up each side in the war.

Axis Powers		Allies
a. Germany	d.	United States
b. Italy	e.	Britain
c. Japan	f.	Soviet Union

23. Essay (10 points)
Theodore Roosevelt and Franklin D. Roosevelt both served as President of the United States. Write a one-paragraph essay describing the reforms made by these two Presidents while in office.
Possible response:
Both Presidents made reforms designed to make America a better place to live. Theodore Roosevelt's reforms included the Interstate Commerce Commission, the Pure Food and Drug Act, and the Meat Inspection Act. He also was involved in the conservation movement. Franklin Roosevelt's reforms included the Civilian Conservation Corps (CCC) and the Works Progress Administration (WPA). He also was involved in making unions legal, setting a minimum wage, establishing Social Security, and building hydroelectric dams.

Individual Performance Task
Graph It!

In this activity you will use the facts at the right to make a line graph about unemployment in the United States. Then you will use your graph to answer some questions.

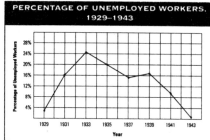

PERCENTAGE OF UNEMPLOYED WORKERS, 1929–1943

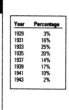

Year	Percentage
1929	3%
1931	16%
1933	25%
1935	20%
1937	14%
1939	17%
1941	10%
1943	2%

Source: U.S. Department of Commerce, Bureau of the Census, *Historical Statistics of the United States from Colonial Times to 1970*, Volume 1

1. What effect did the stock market crash have on unemployment in the United States?
Possible response: It caused unemployment to rise.

2. What effect did the New Deal have on unemployment in the United States?
Possible response: It caused unemployment to fall slightly.

3. What effect did World War II have on unemployment in the United States?
Possible response: It caused unemployment to fall a lot.

Group Performance Task
Billboard Advertising

A billboard along a highway or street is designed to advertise a product, a service, or a cause to the people passing by. Most people have only 10 to 15 seconds to read a billboard. In this task your group will design and make a mural-size billboard that might have been used in World War II.

Step 1 Each person in your group should do research on one of the following billboard ideas:
- a billboard to get men or women to join one branch of the military (The military branches in World War II were the Army, Army Air Corps, Navy, Marines, and Coast Guard. Each branch of the military had a special unit for women.)
- a billboard to support rationing
- a billboard encouraging security and secrecy
- a billboard on women in the workforce
- a billboard on buying bonds to finance the war

Step 2 As a group, select the topic you want to use for the billboard.

Step 3 As a group, decide what words and pictures will be on your billboard. Remember that you must get your message across in a very brief period of time. Look at billboards in your area to see how they use just a few words to get their messages across.

Step 4 Make a rough sketch of your mural-size billboard. Then use watercolors or markers to make a final copy. Display your billboard where others can see it.

ANSWERS

Chapter Test 19

Part One: Test Your Understanding (4 points each)

DIRECTIONS: Use the words or names from the box below to complete the sentences that follow.

airlift	César Chávez	Cold War
hawks	inflation	integration
missiles	Richard M. Nixon	nonviolent
Rosa Parks	Ronald Reagan	segregation
South Vietnam	superpowers	

1. In the years after World War II, the United States and the Soviet Union became the world's **superpowers**.

2. When the Soviet Union blocked supplies from getting to Berlin, the Allies used an **airlift** to take food and fuel to the city.

3. The United States blockaded Cuba when the Soviet Union placed **missiles** on the island.

4. In 1954 the Supreme Court ordered an end to **segregation** in public schools.

5. The Montgomery, Alabama, bus boycott was started when **Rosa Parks** refused to give up her seat on a bus to a white man.

6. Marches and boycotts are examples of **nonviolent** protest to bring about change.

(continued)

---

7. The bringing together of all races in education, jobs, and housing is called **integration**

8. **César Chávez** formed the United Farm Workers to win better wages and conditions for farm workers.

9. In the Vietnam War, the United States fought on the side of **South Vietnam**.

10. The costs of the Vietnam War and the Great Society programs led to **inflation** in the U.S. economy.

11. **Hawks** were Americans who supported the Vietnam War at any cost.

12. **Richard M. Nixon** was the first United States President to resign from office.

13. In 1985 President **Ronald Reagan** met with Soviet leader Mikhail Gorbachev to discuss the "cause of world peace."

14. When President George Bush referred to "a new world order," he meant a world without the **Cold War**.

(continued)

Part Two: Test Your Skills (24 points)

DIRECTIONS: It is the duty of all United States citizens to act responsibly. Complete the following activities on citizenship.

15. What are four things a student can do to be a responsible citizen?

   Possible responses: help keep the neighborhood clean; mow the lawn for an

   elderly person; recycle old newspapers and cans; collect food for the hungry;

   volunteer to work in a hospital; collect clothing and blankets for the

   homeless; visit with elderly people in a nursing home

16. Describe how civil rights leaders such as Dr. Martin Luther King, Jr. and Rosa Parks acted as responsible citizens to fight injustice.

   Possible responses: Dr. King led peaceful protest marches and made

   speeches; Mrs. Parks refused to give up her seat on a bus.

(continued)

Part Three: Apply What You Have Learned

DIRECTIONS: Complete each of the following activities.

17. **Time Line (10 points)**
   Match the letters on the time line with the events from the list below. Place the correct letter in the space provided.

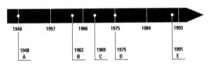

   | 1948 | 1957 | 1966 | 1975 | 1984 | 1993 |

   | 1948 | | 1962 | 1969 | 1975 | | 1991 |
   | A | | B | C | D | | E |

   E breakup of the Soviet Union

   A Berlin Airlift

   B Cuban missile crisis

   C *Apollo 11* mission to the moon

   D Vietnam War ends

18. **Essay (10 points)**
   While he was President, Richard M. Nixon did much to ease Cold War tensions among the United States, China, and the Soviet Union. Write a one-paragraph essay explaining what President Nixon did to ease tensions.

   Possible response:
   President Nixon did much to ease Cold War tensions with China and the Soviet Union. For example, he visited both countries, he increased trade with both countries, he increased scientific and cultural cooperation with both countries, and he negotiated arms-control agreements with the Soviet Union.

ANSWERS

Chapter Test 20

Part One: Test Your Understanding (4 points each)

DIRECTIONS: *Circle the letter of the best answer.*

1. The devaluation of Mexico's money in 1994 made it difficult for Mexico's middle class to
   A. vote in elections.
   B. buy consumer goods.
   C. communicate with people living outside Mexico.
   D. stage peaceful protests against the government.

2. The purpose of NAFTA is to
   A. increase trade among the United States, Canada, and Mexico.
   B. protect the cultures of the American Indians living in North America.
   C. place an embargo on imports into Canada.
   D. bring democracy to the countries of Central and South America.

3. In 1993 the people of Puerto Rico voted to
   A. declare independence from Britain.
   B. become a state of the United States.
   C. become a territory of Britain.
   D. remain a commonwealth of the United States.

4. Fidel Castro is the communist dictator of
   A. the Dominican Republic.
   B. Cuba.
   C. Jamaica.
   D. Brazil.

5. What is the purpose of the United States embargo on Cuba?
   A. It stops the United States from trading its goods with Cuba.
   B. It keeps the Soviet Union from sending missiles to Cuba.
   C. It prevents Cuba from holding free elections.
   D. It allows free trade to develop between Cuba and North America.

6. The United States military helped Jean-Bertrand Aristide return to power in 1994 as president of
   A. Bolivia.
   B. Venezuela.
   C. Haiti.
   D. Chile.

7. Violeta Chamorro ended her country's communist government when she was elected president of
   A. El Salvador.
   B. Nicaragua.
   C. Guatemala.
   D. Mexico.

8. Deforestation is a major problem in
   A. Canada.
   B. Cuba.
   C. Brazil.
   D. Haiti.

9. The main purpose of the OAS is to settle disagreements
   A. between the free world and communist nations.
   B. among nations of the Western Hemisphere.
   C. among nations that fought in World War II.
   D. between the United States and Japan.

10. The Charter of Rights and Freedoms is
    A. an agreement to end communism in all South American countries.
    B. a bill of rights proposed by the Cuban people.
    C. the document that broke up the Soviet Union.
    D. a section that was added to Canada's Constitution of 1982.

11. What was the main effect of the Canadian Constitution of 1982?
    A. It caused a civil war in Canada.
    B. It divided the people of Canada.
    C. It led to closer relations with the government of Britain.
    D. It weakened the economy of Canada.

12. Which of the following Canadian provinces has objected most to the Constitution of 1982?
    A. Alberta
    B. New Brunswick
    C. British Columbia
    D. Quebec

13. Most people who live in Quebec, Canada, are
    A. Mexican Canadians.
    B. British Canadians.
    C. French Canadians.
    D. German Canadians.

14. People in Canada who are separatists want
    A. British Columbia to become a state in the United States.
    B. to end free trade between the United States and Canada.
    C. to limit French language and culture.
    D. Quebec to secede from Canada and become an independent nation.

(continued)

CHAPTER 20 TEST

Assessment Program 163

164 Assessment Program

CHAPTER 20 TEST

(continued)

Part Two: Test Your Skills (15 points)

DIRECTIONS: *Figure A below is a map showing the borders of countries in Central America. Figure B below is a cartogram showing the number of immigrants that came from each country to the United States. Use the information in the map and the cartogram to answer the questions that follow.*

Figure A

Figure B

15. Which country sent the largest number of immigrants to the United States?

    How can you tell? **Mexico; it is the largest country on the cartogram.**

16. Which country sent more immigrants to the United States—El Salvador or Belize?

    How can you tell? **El Salvador; it is larger than Belize on the cartogram.**

17. Which country sent the fewest immigrants to the United States? How can you tell?

    Costa Rica; it is the smallest country on the cartogram.

(continued)

Part Three: Apply What You Have Learned

DIRECTIONS: *Complete each of the following activities.*

18. **Problems and Their Causes (12 points)**
    Describe the cause of each of the problems listed below.

Problems of Nations in the Americas	Causes of Problems
the revolt of farmers in Chiapas, Mexico	Possible response: The farmers in Chiapas revolted because the government of Mexico would not protect their land or their culture from the consequences of the NAFTA agreement.
the conflict to restore democracy in Haiti	Possible response: Jean-Bertrand Aristide, the elected president, had been removed from office by the military in Haiti.
the desire of people in Quebec, Canada, to secede	Possible response: The separatists did not believe that the Constitution of 1982 recognized their special role in Canada. They wanted a veto over national decisions and the right to use the French language only.

19. **Use Vocabulary (7 points)**
    Match the term on the left with the correct description on the right.
    Write the correct number in the space provided.

    a. __4__ deforestation   1. a political region of Canada
    b. __6__ interest rate   2. a person of Indian and European background
    c. __1__ province   3. a kind of territory
    d. __5__ liberate   4. the widespread cutting down of forests
    e. __7__ metropolitan area   5. to set free
    f. __3__ commonwealth   6. what a bank charges to borrow money
    g. __2__ mestizo   7. a city and all the suburbs around it

20. **Essay (10 points)**
    Write a one-paragraph essay describing the special relationship between the United States and Puerto Rico.

    Possible response: Puerto Rico is a commonwealth of the United States. The people of Puerto Rico are United States citizens. They are self-governing and make their own decisions about their government, but they also have close political ties to the government of the United States.

CHAPTER 20 TEST

Assessment Program 165

166 Assessment Program

CHAPTER 20 TEST

ANSWER KEY

Assessment Program 213

ANSWERS

Unit 10 Test

Part One: Test Your Understanding (4 points each)

DIRECTIONS: Circle the letter of the best answer.

1. Which of the following United States Presidents ordered a naval blockade of Cuba during the Cuban missile crisis?
   A. Richard Nixon
   (B.) John F. Kennedy
   C. Ronald Reagan
   D. Jimmy Carter

2. What was the main goal of both the United States and the Soviet Union in the arms race?
   A. to control the entire world
   B. to bring an end to the Berlin crisis
   (C.) to have the most powerful weapons
   D. to start a war in Asia

3. Neil Armstrong was
   (A.) the first person to set foot on the moon.
   B. a U.S. military leader during the Vietnam War.
   C. the lawyer who argued for the desegregation of public schools.
   D. the first U.S. President to visit communist China.

4. Martin Luther King, Jr., thought that the best way to work for civil rights was to
   A. have a complete separation between white people and black people.
   (B.) use nonviolent protest.
   C. use any means necessary.
   D. organize a strike.

5. César Chávez started an organization to
   A. bring an end to the Vietnam War.
   (B.) win better wages and improve working conditions for farmworkers.
   C. work for the right of Indian tribes to run their own businesses and health and education programs.
   D. make sure that all jobs were open to both men and women.

6. President Lyndon Johnson's program to make life better for all Americans was called the
   (A.) Great Society.
   B. New Horizon.
   C. Square Deal.
   D. New Deal.

(continued)

7. Mikhail Gorbachev helped bring about change in the former Soviet Union through his policy of
   A. Québecois.
   B. Nunavut.
   (C.) perestroika.
   D. deforestation.

8. The fall of the Berlin Wall and the breakup of the Soviet Union led to
   A. the United States blockade of Cuba.
   (B.) the end of the Cold War.
   C. the growth of the middle class in Mexico.
   D. the resignation of President Jimmy Carter from office.

DIRECTIONS: Match the description on the left with the term or name on the right. Then write the correct letter in the space provided.

9. __E__ Canadian province that wants to secede from Canada to protect its French culture

10. __C__ free trade agreement between the United States, Canada, and Mexico

11. __F__ amounts that banks charge customers to borrow money

12. __A__ country in which Jean-Bertrand Aristide was elected president

13. __D__ cities and all the suburbs and other population areas around them

14. __B__ group that tries to settle problems between nations in the Western Hemisphere

A. Haiti
B. Organization of American States
C. NAFTA
D. metropolitan areas
E. Quebec
F. interest rates

(continued)

Part Two: Test Your Skills (20 points)

DIRECTIONS: Below are four political symbols of American history and politics. Explain what each symbol is and what it represents.

Symbol	Meaning
15.	Possible response: The Liberty Bell represents freedom and liberty in the United States. It also represents the rights of all citizens.
16.	Possible response: George Washington was the leader in the Revolutionary War and the first President of the United States. He represents the ideals of leadership and patriotism.
17.	Possible response: The Statue of Liberty represent freedom and the warm welcome that people immigrating to the United States receive.
18.	Possible response: Abraham Lincoln, the sixteenth President of the United States, represents honesty and national unity.

(continued)

Part Three: Apply What You Have Learned

DIRECTIONS: Complete each of the following activities.

19. Which One Does Not Belong? (8 points)
    Listed below are groups of terms or names. Circle the one that does not belong in each group and explain why.

    hawk   (embargo)   dove

    Possible response: Hawks and doves are people for and against war. Embargo is the United States policy toward trade with Cuba.

    commonwealth   Puerto Rico   (Brazil)

    Possible response: Puerto Rico is a commonwealth of the United States. Brazil is an independent country.

    AIM   United Farm Workers   (OAS)

    Possible response: AIM and UFW are organizations that work for equal rights. The OAS is an international organization of countries in the Western Hemisphere.

    (Fidel Castro)   nonviolence   Martin Luther King, Jr.

    Possible response: Nonviolence was the basis of the policy of Martin Luther King, Jr. Fidel Castro is the dictator of Cuba.

(continued)

20. *Action (6 points)*

Sometimes nations or peoples take strong action to achieve their goals. Listed below are three such actions. Explain the results of each.

Action	Results of the Action
a. Berlin blockade	**Possible response:** The Berlin blockade was the result of Soviet actions to prevent land travel to Berlin. The Allied powers responded by using an airlift to supply food and fuel to the city. The Allied action kept the city free.
b. American blockade of Cuba during the Cuban missile crisis	**Possible response:** When the Soviet Union put missiles in Cuba, the United States sent its navy to blockade the island. This action forced the Soviets to remove their missiles.
c. Mohawk Indians in Quebec, Canada, protested the building of a golf course on their land	**Possible response:** The Mohawks' protests succeeded in stopping the construction on their land.

21. *Essay (10 points)*

Write a one-paragraph essay explaining what caused the Korean War and what the outcome of the war was.

Possible response:
The Korean War was caused when North Korea, backed by the Soviet Union, invaded South Korea. The outcome of the war was that South Korea, with United States help, remained a free and independent country.

Individual Performance Task
Stamp It Out!

A postage stamp has a value stated in numbers, an illustration, and often the name of a country and a title or an explanation. In this task you will make a postage stamp (on an 8½-inch-by-11-inch sheet of paper) that honors one of the following people or events:

- the Berlin Airlift
- the end of the Cold War
- the actions of Rosa Parks
- the end of the Vietnam War
- the passage of NAFTA

Step 1 Select one of the topics above for the subject of a postage stamp or, with your teacher's approval, select a topic from this unit. Use materials in the textbook or do research in your school library to learn more about your topic.

Step 2 Make a rough sketch of a postage stamp. Show it to a classmate and ask whether it is clear and understandable.

Step 3 Make improvements in the rough sketch. Then make a final copy.

Step 4 Display the final copy of the postage stamp where others can see it.

Group Performance Task
Eyewitness News

In a television news story one or more reporters will talk to one or more people who have taken part in some event. The news story usually has an introduction, an interview with a person or persons, and a conclusion. In this task your group will prepare a news story as though it were to be broadcast on a television news program.

Step 1 Select one of the following topics for a news story or, with the approval of your teacher, select your own topic. Decide which role each member of the group will take.

Topic	Roles
Berlin Airlift	a reporter, a citizen of Berlin, and an Air Force pilot
Vietnam War	a reporter, two hawks, and two doves
Canadian separatists	a reporter, a person opposed to the separatists, and a person in favor of the separatists
Puerto Rico's relationship to the United States	a reporter, a person who wants Puerto Rico to be a state, a person who wants Puerto Rico to remain a commonwealth, and a person who wants Puerto Rico to be an independent country
the struggle for equal rights	a reporter, a person from AIM, a person from the United Farm Workers, and a person from NOW

Step 2 Use the textbook and library resources to learn more about your topic. The members of the group should try to find information that is close to what they would say if they were on a television news program.

Step 3 As a group, make a rough outline of the questions the reporter will ask and the answers that the others will give. Each person in the group will have specific things to say.

Step 4 Practice the news story. Time the story with a watch to determine how long it will take to present to the class. All members of the group should memorize what they are going to say.

Step 5 Have at least one complete dress rehearsal of the news story presentation.

Step 6 Present the news story to the rest of the class. Act as though you were on a live television program.